ADVANCE PRAISE

"A gutsy and profound book. Those who crave the truth will inhale *The Flipside of Feminism*, while those beholden to feminism will resist it. For both, *Flipside* is a must-read. Schlafly and Venker show how insidious the feminist movement is—and what is its real motive."　**—Ann Coulter**

"*The Flipside of Feminism* exposes the lies at the core of the feminist agenda: there is no difference between men and women, the hook-up culture is liberating, women are oppressed victims in the home and office, and children are fine when left all day in daycare. Those who consider themselves 'socially liberal but fiscally conservative' will re-examine their attitudes after reading this book."　**—Mark Levin**

"My friend Phyllis Schalfly has been a tireless warrior against the feminists' ongoing cultural assaults on this nation and refuses to allow their attacks to proceed under the radar while so many other important issues consume our attention and energy. Phyllis and Suzanne Venker have written a powerful exposé on the feminists' war on traditional values and, ultimately, on the true value of women and family. In *The Flipside of Feminism* they provide a practical guide for reclaiming what should never have been lost."
—David Limbaugh

"Phyllis Schlafly and Suzanne Venker have written a courageous and illuminating book on the oppression of women by the feminist left. Everyone of sound mind should read and learn from this book."　**—David Horowitz**

"*The Flipside of Feminism* is a book that speaks truths we all know in our heart but often don't know how to express or whether to express. Suzanne Venker and Phyllis Schlafly speak boldly and wisely against the vapid conventional wisdom of contemporary feminism. An enjoyable, illuminating read!"　**—Dinesh D'Souza**, *New York Times* bestselling author

"Radical feminists have imposed their destructive agenda on our families and institutions, as convincingly detailed in this call to arms by Suzanne Venker and the indispensable Phyllis Schlafly. *The Flipside of Feminism* is an eye-opening expose that will recruit many to their cause."
—Kate O'Beirne, president of National Review Institute and
author of the *NY Times* bestseller *Women Who Make the World Worse
and How Their Radical Feminist Assault Is Ruining Our Schools,
Families, Military, and Sports*

"When the poisonous dust of the past forty years has settled, and the world's healthiest, wealthiest, and most privileged women stop making themselves—and the men and children in their lives—miserable in their angry pursuit of what has so falsely been called "woman power," they will have owed an immeasurable debt to Phyllis Schlafly, for she has bravely held her ground since the feminist movement first began. And now, decades later, she has joined forces with Suzanne Venker to provide for women a road map—missing not a single road-marker or monument—and promises the straightest route to what will once again make women strong."

—**Midge Decter**,
founder of the Independent Women's Forum and author of
An Old Wife's Tale: My Seven Decades in Love and War

"Feminism has hurt men and women, children, and marriage—that's the flipside of feminism. So what do we do about it? Phyllis Schlafly and Suzanne Venker offer a cultural handbook to pick up the pieces left in the wake of the feminist movement." —**Kathryn Jean Lopez**,
editor at large, National Review Online,
& nationally syndicated columnist

"*The Flipside of Feminism* helps us understand that portion of feminism that demonizes men, discounts dads, undervalues the family, and encourages women to see themselves as victims—none of which can accurately be called "progress." Where feminism focuses on the lemons in women's lives, *Flipside* provides the recipe for lemonade. Now that's progress."

—**Dr. Warren Farrell**,
author of the international bestseller *The Myth of Male Power*

"NOW and Women's Studies departments speak for some women, but on sex, family, day care, and much else, Venker and Schlafly speak for far more."

—**Dr. Steven E. Rhoads**,
public policy professor and author of
Taking Sex Differences Seriously

"Buckle your seat belts, book club mavens. *Flipside* is brilliant! Will turn your concept of feminism upside down." —**Doris Wild Helmering**,
psychotherapist, former advice columnist, and author of
Happily Ever After and *Husbands, Wives, and Sex*

THE
FLIPSIDE
OF
FEMINISM

What Conservative Women Know—
and Men Can't Say

SUZANNE VENKER
and PHYLLIS SCHLAFLY

WND Books

THE FLIPSIDE OF FEMINISM
WND Books

Published by WorldNetDaily
Washington, D.C.

Copyright © 2011
Phyllis Schlafly and Suzanne Venker

Written by Phyllis Schlafly and Suzanne Venker
Jacket design by Mark Karis
Interior design by Neuwirth & Associates, Inc.

WND Books are distributed to the trade by:
Midpoint Trade Books
27 West 20th Street, Suite 1102
New York, NY 10011

WND Books are available at special discounts for bulk purchases. WND Books, Inc. also publishes books in electronic formats. For more information call (541-474-1776) or visit www.wndbooks.com.

ISBN 13 Digit: 978-1-935071-27-3
Library of Congress information available

Printed in the United States of America

10 9 8 7 6 5 4 3 2 1

For Suzanne's husband, Bill,
who always knew his feminist professors were nuts.

And for all young women who've been made to feel out of step.

I owe nothing to women's lib.

—Margaret Thatcher

Feminism has much to answer for denigrating men and encouraging women to seek independence whatever the cost to their families. It's time to puncture the myth.

—Rebecca Walker,
daughter of *The Color Purple*'s Alice Walker

I would rather tell you the truth and have you be upset, than lie to you and have you lose respect for my integrity. You may not like what I say. However, if you do get offended, you will have to work that out on your own.

—Andre Harper, author of *Political Emancipation*

CONTENTS

This is a book about the effect left-wing women have had on American society. The ideology of this group is unlike most Americans in that it is steeped in feminist dogma, which now governs the dialogue and narrative in almost every sector of American life because women on the left hold so much power.

As a result of their influence, women and men on both sides of the political aisle have trouble making sense of where, if at all, feminism fits into their lives. Many qualify their position by distinguishing among different *kinds* of feminism. Some people argue that feminism deserves the credit for the freedoms and opportunities women enjoy today, but since we've now achieved equality we don't need feminism anymore. Other people support the assertion that feminism has three classifications: first wave (the nineteenth-century suffragettes), second wave (1960s feminists), and third wave (today's feminists).

Some have even tried to rehabilitate feminism by claiming conservative women belong to something called the "new feminism," or even "pro-life feminism" (Sarah Palin comes to mind)—as if there were such a thing. As rising star Dana Loesch wrote in the *Washington Examiner,* "It should surprise no one that many conservative women are bucking the notion that liberalism owns the patent on 'feminism.' . . . The *liberal* idea of feminism has failed."[1]

The Flipside of Feminism puts an end to the confusion about feminism's role in our lives. While the book has been a joint effort throughout, Suzanne alone wrote the introduction. We share her story as a backdrop to the modern generation's allegiance to the feminist movement.

THE
FLIPSIDE
OF
FEMINISM

CONSERVATIVE TRAILBLAZERS
by Suzanne Venker

> Being on the left is a no-brainer. You don't have to do anything to be on the left. You just have to keep your mouth shut and go along with the crowd.
>
> — Jon Voight

I've been labeled conservative ever since I can remember—and it wasn't meant as a compliment. Liberalism was sweeping the nation when I came of age, so being conservative was decidedly uncool. Most of my contemporaries were raised by baby-boomer parents who instilled in their children a left-wing view of the world, but my parents hailed from the Greatest Generation (those who lived through the Great Depression). Thus, I was raised with a different set of values.

Admittedly, I didn't always like having older parents (as my mother will confirm); but today I am grateful, for their wisdom has served me well. While the "cool" parents were less strict and seemingly more fun, many taught their children—either directly or indirectly—a jaded view of men, women, and society. I didn't get any of that.

I was raised in the heartland in an upscale suburb of St. Louis, Missouri. I suppose my family would be considered upper middle class, but don't tell my mother that. To her, wealth of any kind is not something to talk about or flaunt. She believes that any extra money a person accumulates in life is to be saved and invested—not spent. In fact, she takes the concept of saving to a fare-thee-well.

That's why my mother cannot spend a dime on anything that isn't absolutely necessary. Going out to lunch when there is food in the refrigerator? That's wasteful. Shopping? Only if your clothes have holes in them. Headed to the bookstore when there's a perfectly good library a block away? Ridiculous. My mother is so tight with money that when I head over to her house after I've dropped off my kids at school, I have to think twice about stopping at Starbucks. It would be futile to tell her I drink most of my coffee (and eat most of my lunches) at home because she'll remember the ten times I bought coffee during the last year and chalk it up as extravagant.

While my mother's frugality is challenging to deal with, I understand it. She is a product of the Great Depression. Her father lost his job when she was young, and my grandmother had to go to work to put food on the table—literally. They even had to move from St. Louis to California to live temporarily with my grandmother's uncle. My grandparents never owned a house, and my mother's primary mode of transportation was either her bicycle or the streetcar. Three generations lived in a small, three-bedroom apartment with one bathroom and no air-conditioning.

I can't tell you how many life lessons my mother drilled into my head over the years as a result of her early life. "Your grandmother could stretch a dime into a dollar," she'd say, replete with hand gestures to drive home the point. "She'd serve roast beef on Sunday and make it last an entire week." Most of my mother's mantras had to do with money and sacrifice—such as, "A bird in the hand is worth two in the bush." My all-time favorite, the one I heard the most growing up, was, "When life hands you lemons, make lemonade."

My parents were forever making lemonade. Neither responded to problems by drinking too much, taking anti-depressants, overeating, or suggesting they were victims. In fact, I can't recall a single day my parents slept in—the way many of us might when life throws a wrench in our plans. My parents were (*are* in the case of my mother—my father died in 2008) unfailingly resilient people, capable of waking up each day with a positive attitude, a new resolve to make things better. Part of this was due to their personalities, but it was also because of the generation in which they were raised. In their day, such optimism was necessary in order to keep from becoming over-whelmed with the challenges of daily life. Maxims were needed to remind people of what they *did* have, as opposed to what they didn't. Wallowing in self-pity, wasting time, and whining about the state of the world was not an option in our house. Neither was resting on one's laurels. The expectation was clear: work hard and persevere, and you will succeed.

Sadly, this is not the message I gleaned from society. America became more and more liberal as I grew up. And the more liberal it became, the more unsettled I felt. By the time I went to Boston University in the mid-1980s, I felt particu-larly alone. Fortunately, I make friends easily and like to have fun (imagine: being conservative *and* having fun!), so that was never a problem. But I was clearly viewed as "that conservative girl from the Midwest."

Most of my friends hailed from the East Coast, and we approached life somewhat differently. While I had not been raised in a particularly religious household (and neither had my friends, unless they were Jewish), I had developed strong belief in right and wrong, and I wasn't afraid to share those beliefs.

I also set limits on my behavior. I didn't use hard drugs, for example (though I drank and smoked a fair amount—in those days, smoking wasn't considered the evil it is today), and I generally retired before midnight and got a lot of flack for it. My friends were a carefree bunch to be sure, but I never considered that unusual or even bad. That's just the way things were back then.

But politics was definitely an issue. Most people I knew voted for Michael Dukakis, while I voted for the first George Bush. And when all my girlfriends attended pro-choice rallies, I stayed behind. Indeed, my alma mater was—and still is—as liberal a university as they come. Students assumed America was a bad place, filled with injustice, inequality, and hypocrisy. They believed it was a country in which people work hard but can't get anywhere because "the man" holds them down.

This attitude was particularly pervasive when it came to women. Though my parents raised me to view the world as my oyster, the culture I found at college viewed women as victims; and the people who were supposed to lift me out of my despair were feminists. "Don't you know feminists are responsible for the freedoms we have today?" my college roommate would ask. As the daughter of a committed feminist, my roommate and I didn't agree on much. "Well, actually," I'd say, "that isn't true." At which point she would look at me as if I had three heads. I think she thought I'd crawled out from under a rock, for she had never heard anyone claim such a thing. No matter how I tried to explain the fallacy of the women's movement, it fell on deaf ears.

It didn't take long before I realized I'd grown up with a different set of values that my contemporaries. I even struggled with my boyfriend (who would later become my husband— and then, duh, ex-husband), who I mistakenly thought shared my values. He was not anti-authority like my other friends— he graduated from Boston University's School of Management for goodness' sake, hardly a bastion of radicals!—and we both became involved in the election of George H. W. Bush. Yet ultimately my boyfriend was as liberal minded as everyone else; I just didn't recognize it at the time. I didn't realize people could vote Republican and still be liberal. Today, this is obvious to me.

I probably should have realized the extent of our differences when we talked about sex. I knew he had "been around the block" a few times, but that wasn't unusual for my generation. I remember chiding him about the number of women—girls, I should say—that he slept with in high school. Whenever we ran into a woman he knew from those earlier days, I'd ask, "So did you sleep with her, too?" Like most good men, he didn't kiss and tell, but his backpedaling gave me the answer. My college sweetheart was an attractive, fun, and charismatic guy who bought into liberal ideology—so much so that he thought it odd I *hadn't* slept around in high school. I think he thought it was cute. He didn't know any women who didn't engage in casual sex. "It's no big deal. Friends have sex all the time," he would say.

In addition to my supposed frigidity, I was different from my girlfriends in another way. They didn't give any thought to marriage and motherhood when making decisions about their lives, whereas I *assumed* marriage and motherhood would be the center of my life. Thus, I chose a career—at that time, it was teaching—that would best accommodate motherhood. I always knew I would work outside the home, but I never expected my career to become my life. That, I suppose, was when the conservative labeling began. For if I wasn't a feminist downgrading the role of wife and mother and planning an exciting career to liberate me from the home, well, then I must be a conservative. That begs the question, where does conservatism fit in when it comes to women's independence?

According to the media elite (the mainstream newspapers, magazines, and television networks that set the news agenda), conservatism has no place in the discussion of female empowerment. When women in the media—most of whom are committed feminists—discuss the state of women in America, it is always from a left-wing perspective. They talk endlessly about their debt to the "women who came before us"—feminist trailblazers—and have convinced women, even conservative women, that feminists are responsible for the freedoms and opportunities women enjoy today.

In a lengthy report by the Center for American Progress (which we discuss in Chapter 1), journalist Maria Shriver wrote about the state of America with respect to women's changing roles. She said, "My mother was . . . a trailblazer for American women. . . . She didn't buy into the propaganda of her day that women had to be soft and submissive and take a back seat. . . . My mother understood power and wanted it. . . . All her heroes were women. . . . She told me their stories, because she wanted me to appreciate the gift and the power of women to change the language, the tempo, and the character of the world."[1]

The assumption behind language like Shriver's—which is standard fare in the media—is that it takes a *liberal* woman (or a Democrat, or a feminist) to be strong, independent, and successful. Feminists love Nancy Pelosi, for example, but they hate Sarah Palin, despite the fact that both women represent the feminist version of "having it all." No committed left-winger sings the praises of conservative women such as Dr. Laura Schlessinger, Michelle Malkin, Sarah Palin, Michele Bachmann, or even Margaret Thatcher—despite the fact that they have, or have had, it all. That's why the so-called women's movement (a misleading term, for it suggests all women are on the same page) is bogus. The feminist movement was never about supporting all women, just liberal women. It was not designed to level the playing field; it was designed to rearrange society to make life more suitable to feminists. It was designed "to change the language, the tempo, and the character of the world."

Here's a twist: What if you're a woman who isn't "soft and submissive"—but thinks America is pretty great? What if you're a strong, independent woman, as feminists claim women should be, but don't believe women are victims? My mother was a trailblazer. She received a master's degree from Radcliffe College in 1952. And trust me: no one could accuse my mother of being "soft," "submissive," or "taking a back seat." On the contrary, she was brave enough to enter the male-dominated world of stock traders—at Merrill Lynch, in the 1950s. When she faced blatant sexism, she didn't whine about it or give up; she went to work at G. H. Walker (another investment bank), where the men were happy to have her. "People who succeed do not expect every company to reward fairly; they *screen for* companies that will recognize their contribution," wrote Warren Farrell, Ph.D. in *The Myth of Male Power.*[2]

Indeed, smart women forge ahead in the face of adversity— they don't stop to complain about being mistreated. As my mother always told me, "There will always be people who want to drag you down. Don't let them." She stayed with G. H. Walker for sixteen years before quitting to stay home with my sister and me.

But my mother is conservative.

In fact, so are all the women in my family, and they are all strong, educated women. Even my *grandmother* got her BA from a great co-ed university in 1920. But to hear the media tell it, you'd think liberal women are the only ones who ever went to college and made something of their lives.

What separates the conservative women in my family from women like Eunice Kennedy is that the women in my family weren't born into privilege. They know what it means to work hard and do without, and this experience usually leads to conservatism. Conservative women don't have a beef with America. They don't want to band together with a bunch of women and try to "change the language, tempo, and the character of the world." They are independent by nature, and their worldview is one of duty, honor, sacrifice, and gratitude.

When life hands you lemons, make lemonade.

I had another advantage over my contemporaries: Phyllis Schlafly is my mother's sister (and only sibling). As the premier anti-feminist of the twentieth century, Phyllis is best known for her fight against the 1970s Equal Rights Amendment. Sounds shocking, doesn't it? What kind of woman would be *against* women's rights? That's how feminists operate: They use benign terminology—*women's rights, reproductive rights, violence against women*—to appeal to people's emotions and marginalize those who disagree, making them sound backward or provincial.

But Phyllis is not a follower, and she wasn't intimidated—which meant I was exposed to an alternative view of women's issues from a very young age. It was like watching Fox News instead of CBS: when most people were taught to think one way, I was presented with a different view. Phyllis's work demonstrated to me early on that feminism is a lie; and the combination of her life's work and my mother's example was the reason I didn't end up like so many modern women: guilt-ridden, stressed out, and saddled with a psychological need to prove my importance in the world.

Perhaps the reason Phyllis is unflappable in the face of feminist attacks is that she worked her way through college, forty-eight hours a week *on the night shift*, firing .30 and .50 caliber ammunition to test it for acceptance by the government. After receiving her BA, she went to graduate school at Harvard, where she received an MA in political science in 1945. That's not to suggest Phyllis is any better than anyone else, but it does prove one thing: any woman who's willing to put in the effort to become successful will be.

And Phyllis *is* successful, which is another reason why she is subject to feminist attacks. Feminists don't believe women can be successful in "the patriarchy"—and to any extent they are, they must owe it to the feminist movement. But Phyllis achieved success and a national following *before* the feminist movement got off the ground. She wrote and self-published her first book, *A Choice Not an Echo*, in 1964 and sold an amazing three million copies. While most women—most *people*—are not as ambitious as Phyllis (at eighty-six, she still works around the clock), her story proves that no one's stopping women if they want to achieve that level of success.

Still, the decision to co-author a book with Phyllis was not easy. Not only was I worried about the nepotism charge (I had never worked with Phyllis in any way, nor have I asked her to do anything on my behalf), Phyllis is a staunch conservative. I knew that by asking her to co-author this book with me, I'd experience guilt by association, and I wasn't sure I wanted to go there. Unlike Phyllis, I'm not what you'd call a loyal conservative. I'm more of an independent conservative, if there is such a thing.

To be perfectly honest, I haven't always wanted people to know I'm Phyllis' niece. I remember her name coming up once during a course I took in college. Though I don't recall what my professor said about her, I can assure you it was neither positive nor polite. Apparently my classmates agreed with the professor's low opinion of Phyllis (their feminist mothers had tutored them well) because they all rolled their eyes and chuckled—at which point I promptly sank down in my chair.

I am no longer sinking down in my chair.

Whether or not you (or more likely, your mother) agree with Phyllis Schlafly's politics, one thing is indisputable: Phyllis knew feminism was a farce long before other folks wised up.

She also knew there were plenty of female role models who did not toe the feminist line. "For a woman to find her identity in the modern world, the path should be sought from the positive women who have found the road and possess the map, rather than from those who have not," she wrote in her book *The Power of the Positive Woman*. She penned those words in 1977—after she had had six children and before she received a law degree from Washington University Law School.[3]

What makes Phyllis a good role model for today's conservatives is that she wasn't afraid to speak the truth in the face of liberal media domination—and she was pilloried as a result. It took enormous courage to stand up to the women in the media at that time. Remember: this was *before* Fox News, talk radio, and the Internet. Phyllis knew all about media bias before it became mainstream—and like Sarah Palin, she was attacked, demeaned, and ridiculed. The media will do whatever they can to undermine the conservative cause, especially when confronted with strong, traditional-minded women.

Phyllis and I have something else in common: I, too, know what it's like to be on the receiving end of feminist bias. I published my first book, *7 Myths of Working Mothers*, in 2004. In it I address the natural conflict between having young children and demanding careers. Not surprisingly, the media were not happy about it. Carol Lin, an anchor on CNN at the time, told me my book "stirred up all the women at CNN." *Glamour* magazine categorized my book as a "Don't" in its "Dos and Don'ts" section—right below *The War on Choice*, a pro-abortion book the editors strongly recommended.

When it comes to speaking your mind in America, the message is clear: you'd better be politically correct (a feminist) or beware. Never say what the media don't want to hear, or they will come after you with a vengeance.

Fortunately, conservative women have strong constitutions. That's because their beliefs are grounded in common sense, wisdom, and independent thought. Modern women bring a unique spin to conservatism. The packaging may be different (house dresses and heels are out; workout garb and sneakers are in), but the brand is the same.

It is our sincere hope that this book helps support Americans who don't believe women in this country are oppressed, who know government is not the solution to women's problems, who don't believe marriage and motherhood are outdated institutions, who think men are *as important as* women, who think gender roles are good and exist for a reason, and who see the mainstream media for who they are.

You don't have to agree with everything in these pages—conservatives can take it if you disagree with them—you just have to be open-minded enough to entertain a different perspective. And that perspective is this: you *can* be a strong, powerful, and even liberated woman—and still be conservative.

I've known this all along. It's time America knew it, too.

· 1 ·

BRAINWASHED

When a crowd adopts a point of view en masse, all critical thinking stops.

—William Powers

When it comes to women in America, *progress* is the operative word. According to the *Free Online Dictionary*, progress means "steady improvement, as of a society or civilization." It's a relative term—how to improve something is entirely subjective. Yet when we talk about women in America, *progress* is never defined, debated, or qualified. The topic is misleading right out of the gate.

For the past several decades, it has been widely accepted that women in America usually, if not always, get the short end of the stick. According to feminists, women, like blacks, have been oppressed for centuries. We're told not enough progress has been made and that society still hasn't leveled the playing field. This philosophy is so embedded in our culture that Americans don't question it. We don't even label it "feminist" to think this way; it's just commonplace to believe women suffer discrimination. Turn on the television, flip through a magazine, or search America's airwaves, and you'll be deluged with stories about women who wonder how their needs can best be met, how they can balance their lives better, or how they can deal with the myriad of problems and dangers they face. Women's grievances dominate the conversation.

But grievances are like crabgrass: the more heat they get, the more it spreads. And that is precisely what has happened with modern women. Feminist organizations even promote the growth of grievances by consciousness-raising sessions, where feminists exchange tales of how badly some man treated them and what government's role should be as compensation. (See the NOW Resolutions on the Equal Rights Amendment in Appendix C.)

In the meantime, buried beneath the surface lies the truth: American women are the most fortunate human beings who have ever lived. No one has it better. No one.

This is a new twist to an old debate, one that elicits shock. It even *sounds* wrong on a piece of paper or rolling off the tongue. That's because Americans have been conditioned to believe otherwise. Millions of Americans think progress requires women's *liberation*—from men, from children, from society's constructs, from just about anything that makes women feel morally obligated to someone or something other than themselves. The saddest part of this misguided view of human nature is that it hasn't made women any happier. In fact, it has done just the opposite. According to a 2007 report from the National Bureau of Economic Research, "As women have gained more freedom, more education, and more power, they have become *less* happy."[1]

The authors of this report, Betsey Stevenson and Justin Wolfers, suggest that "the salience of the women's movement fueled elation in the 1970s that has dissipated in the ensuing years."[2] That isn't surprising. Most women in America are a right-of-center bunch and don't want what women on the left want. The majority of women in this country are traditionalists and don't want to change America.

Feminists do. They've spent decades trying to convince women that America needs to accommodate them so women can be unshackled, free, and presumably happy. It has been an alluring concept. Certainly women like the *idea* of being free from their responsibilities from time to time; they may like the *thought* of being liberated from husbands and children occasionally. Who wouldn't? Marriage and motherhood require a lot of work and sacrifice. But women don't want to be "free" if being free means being single, dependent on the government, or even being a big-shot powerhouse with no time for family. Most women in America want what any reasonable person wants: a family to love and—yes—even depend on.

The female left wants something else. "As we approach a new century—and a new millennium—it's the men who have to break through to a new way of thinking about themselves and society," wrote Betty Friedan in the 2001 edition of her 1963 landmark book, *The Feminine Mystique*. "Too bad women can't do it for them, or go much further without them. Because it's awesome to consider how women have changed the possibilities of our lives since we broke through the feminine mystique only two generations ago."[3]

Those powerful words helped to shape a generation of American women. Implicit in Friedan's worldview—the worldview so many Americans have been raised to accept—is the notion that women are oppressed, and that men are the ones who need to change. Friedan believed the odds are severely stacked against women. The only way to eliminate female oppression, she said, is to change men and society—to create a different America, one that's more fair and just to women.

Those who are tempted to write off Betty Friedan as a has-been shouldn't. Her words live on in the minds of influential female leftists whose goals are no different from Friedan's. In November 2009, Maria Shriver, along with the left-wing think tank Center for American Progress, produced an exhaustive, four-hundred-page document titled *The Shriver Report: A Woman's Nation Changes Everything*. Its fundamental argument is that government policies and laws "continue to rely on an outdated model of the American family."[4]

Shriver and company—which includes Oprah Winfrey—seek to remedy this supposed problem by proving we are no longer living in a "man's world" but are now living in a "woman's world." They consider the traditional family a thing of the past, which is fine with them because what feminists really want is a matriarchy. And now they've admitted it. *The Shriver Report* boasted, "As we move into this phase we're calling a woman's nation, women can turn their pivotal role as wage-earners, as consumers, as bosses, as opinion-shapers, as co-equal partners in whatever we do into a potent force for change. Emergent economic power gives women a new seat at the table—at the head of the table."[5]

Every couple of years *Time* and *Newsweek* ask, "Is Feminism Dead?" It is not dead. While people associate feminism with the 1960s revolution, since that is when feminism began, feminism and feminists didn't disappear just because they're no longer marching in the streets. They simply chucked the loud protests and morphed into the fabric of society. The left offered feminists a home, a place where they could comfortably hang out—along with the Barack Obamas of the world—and plot their strategy to "fundamentally transform" America.

We're not exaggerating. *The Shriver Report* was delivered to *each* of the Fortune 500 CEOs, all 535 members of Congress, and President Obama, who responded, "When I think about policy, I'm constantly thinking about how we can provide more resources so women can thrive."[6]

If feminism appears to be dead, that's only because the media seldom use the term *feminist*. This makes feminism appear mainstream, rather than a fringe movement.

On college campuses throughout America, however, feminism *is* mainstream. Courses in Women's Studies abound, and millions of impressionable women take them. But notice they don't call these classes Feminist Studies (which would be the accurate title) because the term *women* suggests that all women think alike—or should think alike. (That's also why the phrase "women's movement" is preferred over "feminist movement.") Yet Women's Studies classes do not appeal to most women—they are nothing more than feminist indoctrination. The professors teach that gender is not a fact of nature, or biologically determined, but a social or environmental construct created by old-fashioned stereotyped training. They consider it a given that women have been subordinated and discriminated against by an unjust male patriarchy and need government action by legislatures and courts to give women their rights.

Some universities come right out and admit their bias. A course at the University of Missouri asserts that U.S. institutions—especially the media, the legal system, and the medical profession—exert social control over women's bodies to promote gender inequalities. Missouri University courses attack femininity as "a tool of self-oppression,"[7] and courses are frankly described as "a training course for radical feminists in radical feminism."[8]

The Women's Studies department at Miami University in Ohio also makes clear that its courses are organized around radical feminist theory. To earn a degree in Women's Studies, the first requirement for the senior thesis is that it "must incorporate feminist perspectives."[9] Typical readings assigned at the University of Arizona are: *Capitalist Patriarchy and the Case for Socialist Feminism, Sexual Democracy: Women, Oppression and Revolution,* and *The Radical Future of Liberal Feminism.*

What happens after college students take these courses? Many women become dismayed or confused. After all, the title

Women's Studies sounds innocuous—students thought they were going to study things that are important, or of interest to them, such as the history of women's role in society, marriage, work, motherhood, and women's achievements. They didn't realize they were walking into a lion's den where disgruntled female professors would fill their heads with left-wing propaganda.

That's what Megan Basham suggests happened to her. In her 2009 book, *Beside Every Successful Man*, the author wrote about wanting to depend on her husband's income so she could live a more slow-paced, family-oriented life. Newly married with no children at the time, Basham was conflicted about her desire to do this. She knew she wanted a life that allowed her to be home with her yet-to-be-born children and have the flexibility to pursue whatever other ambitions she might have, but she felt uneasy about being a one-income family since the culture assures her this isn't a realistic goal. "I was worried that if anyone was going to lift us out of living paycheck to paycheck, it was going to be me. And though I could hear the voice of my Women's Studies professor piping up in my head—Well, why shouldn't it be you?—the prospect of it stirred in me a faint but growing bitterness."[10]

Feminist bias on campus isn't relegated to Women's Studies classes—most liberal arts programs espouse this same ideology, so men get an earful as well. And when universities welcome female speakers to their campus, they're usually feminists. College student Lauren Rhodes attended one such lecture. At nineteen, Rhodes felt strongly about her choice to buck the status quo and wait until she met "the one" to have sex. Unfortunately, she attended a lecture by feminist author and blogger Jessica Valenti. Rhodes didn't realize what a feminist really is. She was under the impression that Valenti would empower her to stick to her guns and do what she felt was best for her as a woman.

By the end of the lecture, Rhodes was despondent and angry. Valenti had spent the better part of an hour telling young people that women should feel free to sleep around without censure. The only reason some women are reticent to engage in one-night stands is because conservatives consider chastity something to aspire to, or they tell women casual sex is dangerous. That's a scare tactic, she said, used to hold women down and keep them virginal.

Basham's and Rhodes' stories are textbook examples of how American women have been taught to think in a manner that goes against their values. The current feminist culture has been so unrelenting and insidious that it's impossible for women to avoid the pressure. Everywhere they turn—from their baby boomer mothers, to their college professors, to their female bosses, to the women in the media—they're bombarded with feminist rhetoric and assumptions.

Today's women have been raised in a society that encourages them to do what they think will make *them* happy. It's a trend that belies common sense, wisdom, and a basic sense of fairness. It is also in stark contrast to the way previous generations of women were raised, yet it stuck. The notion of the good of the family—a decidedly conservative philosophy—has been supplanted by the left-wing view of being true to oneself. "The feminist message for women is inextricably linked to the individualist message," wrote popular speaker and author Dr. Jean Twenge in *Generation Me*.[11]

THIRD WAVE FRINGE FEMINISTS

There are two groups of feminists in America: fringe feminists and elite feminists. Fringe feminists proudly refer to themselves as feminists and label themselves "third wave" in order to distinguish themselves from their baby boomer mothers, who are called "second wave" feminists. These fringe feminists include twenty- and thirty-something women such as Jessica Valenti, who talk endlessly about eradicating sexism. Ms. Valenti repeatedly throws around the word "misogyny" (hatred of women) and is forever telling American women they're oppressed: "We act as if the hatred directed at women is something that can be dealt with by a stern talking to, as if the misogyny embedded in our culture is an unruly child rather than systematic oppression."[12]

Other fringe feminists include women such as authors/activists Jennifer Baumgardner and Amy Richards. While these women have a following, their values will never be embraced by everyday Americans because they're too far to the left. For example, Richards—who lives in Manhattan—wrote a 2004 article for the *New York Times* about discovering she was pregnant with triplets (without the use of fertility drugs). Unmarried (and happily so, since Richards grew up without a father and insists she doesn't miss what she never had), Richards got pregnant with her longtime boyfriend, Peter.

When they went to the obstetrician for an ultrasound and Richards discovered she was carrying triplets, she turned to a doctor and asked, "Is it possible to get rid of one of them? Or two of them?"[13] Richards boldly recounted the episode in a *New York Times* article and described her reaction to the pregnancy. "When I found out about the triplets, I felt like: Now I'm going to have to move to Staten Island. I'll never leave my house because I'll have to care for these children. I'll have to start shopping at Costco and buy big jars of mayonnaise. Even in my moments of thinking about having three, I don't think deep down I was ever considering it."[14]

Richards may be an anomaly even for feminists, but no self-respecting leftist would deny Richards' "right" to an abortion or selective reduction even if it is approached in such a cavalier, offensive manner. That pregnant women can now "consider" whether or not they'd *like* to bring babies into the world is a fait accompli. Yet pro-choice or not, most Americans express shock at the attitude and behavior of women such as Richards. That's why fringe feminists are not the problem.

It's the other group we need to worry about.

THE FEMINIST ELITE

"There is something special that happens when you get a group of powerful women in a room . . . and shut the door."[15] So begins the 2010 book *Secrets of Powerful Women,* a compilation of essays from leftist females, many of whom are politicians. The book is designed to share women's stories of achievement and encourage young women to follow through on their career aspirations. The book claims to represent both political philosophies, but it does no such thing. Out of more than twenty women, only a handful are Republicans—and not just any Republicans, *feminist* Republicans. "A woman's right to control her own body is absolutely central to our success as a civilization. The world's most oppressive regimes target those who would liberate women from the shackles of ignorance or bondage. This includes reproductive 'bondage'—and parallels can be drawn in our own country," wrote Susan Bevan, co-chair of Republican Majority for Choice.[16]

Today's Americans know the media are generally liberal, if not outright leftist. (To put media bias in perspective, during the 2008 election year, 1,160 employees at the three major networks—ABC, NBC, and CBS—contributed more than $1 million dollars to Democratic candidates. By contrast, only 193 employees contributed a total of $142,863 to Republican candidates.) But when we think of media, we often think only of television and radio.

Another arm of liberal bias is the publishing industry, which includes books like *Secrets of Powerful Women*, as well as dozens of women's magazines. They are a significant part of the liberal establishment. Myrna Blyth, former *Ladies' Home Journal* editor, exposed her former colleagues in *Spin Sisters: How the Women of the Media Sell Unhappiness and Liberalism to the Women of America*. She wrote: "Women's magazines, a nearly $7 billion-a-year business, are based on telling women their lives are too tough for them to handle and they should feel very sorry for themselves. This distorted vision of your life is absolutely crazy."[17]

By now, most people understand there's a culture war in America between folks on the right who want to preserve our country's traditions and folks on the left who want to change America, but *feminist* bias is not generally recognized as an essential part of media bias. Yet a significant portion of the left in America is female, and they have convinced Americans that women are victims of an unjust, patriarchal society and must look to the government to redress their grievances.

To give you an idea of how pervasive feminist bias is, consider this comment by best-selling author and former CBS journalist Bernard Goldberg: "I know a few top male producers who would rather walk barefoot on cut glass while drinking Drano than have to face the missus back home after giving the green light to a story on the excesses of feminism."[18]

In addition to their influence over media producers, the feminist elite have another advantage: humans are susceptible to victimhood. Since it's easier to point fingers than to accept blame, it isn't hard for feminists to gather momentum. After Suzanne wrote on her blog a disparaging piece about education secretary Arne Duncan's argument that schools in America should be open "14 hours a day, 7 days a week, 11–12 months of the year," one man commented that allowing mothers to keep their kids in school all the time would be a good thing because it would set them free. He wrote, "Your precious 'American family' is just fine, to the extent that it ever really existed in the first place. I mean, maybe to you it was worth keeping women repressed so they felt trapped in loveless marriages so they could pump out kids for their husband's bloodlines, but I'm fine with people being allowed to be people." This reader clearly sees women as victims of the family institution.

Indeed, feminists have manipulated human nature to their advantage—they know it's easy to get people to succumb to victimhood. That's why, if you ask a feminist to define feminism, she'll give you the standard, bogus answer: "Feminism is about equal rights for women." That benign, but very inaccurate, definition gives people the impression that feminism is a good thing. After all, who doesn't believe in equal rights? But feminism is not about equal rights at all.

Feminism is about power for the female left.

That's why you rarely hear women in the media brag about successful women such as Condoleezza Rice. No matter how rich or prominent or smart or advantaged a woman may be, feminists teach that success is beyond her grasp because institutional sexism holds her down. And when a woman *has* achieved success both in a career and as a wife and mother, feminists feel personally threatened because it proves motherhood isn't oppressive.

When Hillary Clinton lost the Democratic nomination for president to Barack Obama, feminists cried about the unfairness of it all. Gloria Steinem opined on CNN that it is "clear that there is profound sexism." She whined that Hillary couldn't crack the "glass ceiling" because there are "still barriers and biases out there" and bemoaned that women find it "difficult to be competent and successful and be liked."[19] On the contrary, women are not disliked for being competent and successful. They are disliked when they whine about being oppressed—because most Americans know that is bogus.

What separates *elite* feminists from *fringe* feminists is that elite feminists don't refer to themselves as feminists. These women are savvy political players. By avoiding the term, they make the feminist agenda appear mainstream. Some of these women are outspoken (without using the *F* word), and others work behind the scenes to drum up support for their left-wing causes. They "sit on review panels to give federal grants to each other to study things only they care about. Every new law they design comes with hundreds of millions of dollars in feminist pork spending," wrote journalist and author Kate O'Beirne in *Women Who Make the World Worse*.[20] They also oppose grants to researchers who might discover information feminists don't *want* people to know.

What elite feminists do is insidious; that's why they're more dangerous than fringe feminists, who are at least honest about what they stand for. Conversely, elite feminists are stealthy—and they live in such a bubble they honestly believe that what *they* think is what any rational human being would think.

This is the mainspring of liberal media bias. As Bernard Goldberg explains in his 2001 book, *Bias*, liberal bias doesn't equate to a bunch of liberals sitting around plotting how they're going to distort facts and lie to the American people—that would be easy to identify. Media bias is deceptive. It refers to journalists' arrogance and the subtle way they spin the news. These folks don't purposely distort facts; they actually *believe* everyone thinks the same way they do. They can't conceive of the notion that there's an alternative perspective in which to view a topic, particularly when it comes to women. That's why they'll attack the book you're now reading. "Most journalists I've spoken to are in such a fog they don't even think of the National Organization for Women as a liberal special interest group," wrote Goldberg.[21]

Who are the feminist elite? They're professors, lawyers, journalists, writers, judges, actresses, bureaucrats, psychologists, and activists—and they include many familiar names: Maria Shriver, Katie Couric, Marlo Thomas, Whoopi Goldberg, Joy Behar, Hillary Clinton, Nancy Pelosi, Michelle Obama, Ruth Bader Ginsburg, Arianna Huffington, Gloria Steinem, Susan Sarandon, Patricia Ireland, Martha Burk (unsuccessful critic of the Masters Golf Tournament), Susan Faludi, Barbara Walters, Meredith Vieira, Diane Sawyer, Kate Michelman, Eleanor Smeal, Maureen Dowd, Naomi Wolf, Eve Ensler (of the infamous *Vagina Monologues*), Susan Douglas, Linda Hirshman, Carol Evans, and even Oprah. Plus nearly all the women in Hollywood and academia.

What these women have in common is clout, and they believe they know what's best for women. Unfortunately, their entire worldview—about men, sex, work, marriage, motherhood, and politics—is fueled by feminist dogma. (As Gloria Steinem reiterated at a keynote speech at the third annual Women and Power conference, "We had great slogans. Like we're becoming the men we wanted to marry."[22]) Since the feminist elite think they know best, they are vicious toward anyone who believes otherwise. That *Secrets of Powerful Women* includes only feminists as examples of real female achievers tells you all you need to know about the bias of the feminist elite.

Bill O'Reilly is correct: there *is* a culture war in America. But it's not just between conservatives and liberals (or, as he puts it, traditionalists and progressives)—it's also between conservative women and liberal women. As University of Virginia political professor Steven Rhoads has written in his book *Taking Sex*

Differences Seriously, "Women are split between a majority who are traditionally feminine and others who are more like men."[23] The women who are "more like men" are feminists—they have wanted men's lives from the get-go.

The problem is that the majority of women in this country don't have the power—feminists do. And feminists influence liberals *as well as conservatives* to conform to the feminist message. The best definition of feminism was recently offered by Feministing's Jessica Valenti in the *Washington Post:* "Feminism is a structural analysis of a world that oppresses women, an ideology based on the notion that patriarchy exists and that it needs to end."[24]

While this negative view of women and their role in society fails to resonate with the majority of American women (most women in America don't feel oppressed), the feminist elite continue to advance their personal agenda, rather than the agenda of the American people. That's why it's imperative for Americans to realize that feminists are the driving force behind much of the change in this country, and they have a powerful friend in Barack Obama. Unless conservatives recognize and expose the *female left* for what it is—and what it is they're doing—the female left may get what it wants.

And what it wants, as new research proves, doesn't make women happy.

· 2 ·

FEMINISM 101: UNCENSORED

Of all tyrannies, a tyranny sincerely exercised for the good of its victims may be the most oppressive.

—C. S. Lewis

F eminists want people to think feminism began with the nineteenth-century suffragettes, but it didn't. The word *feminist* didn't become boilerplate language until the counter-cultural revolution of the 1960s, when women took to the streets in the name of "equality" and "liberation."

Betty Friedan is credited with being the leader of what is now known as "second wave feminism." It refers to the 1960s feminists who supposedly picked up where the suffragettes left off. In fact, the two groups have nothing in common. The suffragettes fought for (and won in 1920) the right for women to vote in all fifty states, but they were family-oriented women who had no desire to eradicate female nature. They were also resolutely opposed to abortion. The feminists of the 1960s (and later), on the other hand, are not pro-family. In addition to viewing abortion a matter of women's "rights," they see the home as a trap for women.

With the shift from moral obligation to self-fulfillment sweeping the nation, Friedan identified what she called "the problem that has no name": the plight of the suburban housewife, who, according to Friedan, felt caged, lonely, and bored. That was the theme of her 1963 book, *The Feminine Mystique*.

Friedan's book was addressed to the housewives of America, for she thought she understood what their lives were like. A mother of three, Friedan wrote of her life at home this way: "An American woman cannot deny that as a housewife, the world is indeed rushing past her door while she just sits and watches. The terror she feels is real." She also wrote that a housewife's anxiety "can be tranquilized by pills, but her desperation is a warning that her existence is in danger."[1]

That's a serious charge. Did Friedan really tap into something most women in those days felt, as Americans have been led to believe, or did she discover something about herself and her own life? After all, Friedan was no average housewife—she had been involved in Marxist politics prior to getting married.

Many people don't realize that the entire women's movement was predicated on a Marxist view of the world. Feminism is a branch of socialism, or collectivism, which draws on a sociopolitical movement that attempts to create a stateless society in which policy decisions are pursued in the (supposed) best interest of society. Feminism, like communism, depends on hypothesizing an oppressed class. "Feminism found common cause with Communist ideology. Breaking up the family was not incidental but central to that ideology," wrote journalist and author Kathleen Parker in her groundbreaking book *Save the Males*.[2]

Indeed, Betty Friedan was no ordinary woman. She came from an unstable household and walked right into another when she married Carl Friedan. Their marriage was a disaster (both were physically abusive to one another), and the needs of children overwhelmed her. To Friedan, home life was oppressive—so she assumed every mother's home life was oppressive. Rather than try to cope and offer other women solutions for how to cope, Friedan *manufactured* a societal problem. She suggested society is to blame for the plight of the American housewife, who lived, she wrote, in a "comfortable concentration camp."[3] (There's that Marxism again.)

Knowing she couldn't appeal to women by defending Marxism, Friedan took advantage of something to which she knew women could relate: the mental and physical drain of raising young children. In *The Feminine Mystique*, she argued that a woman's devotion to her husband and children is a sacrifice of such magnitude that it inevitably stunts her growth as an individual. Raising children, Friedan argued, is a thankless pursuit that doesn't allow women to use their intelligence in a manner that benefits society. She had no appreciation for the economic advantage to any society when mothers, out of sheer duty and love, perform the awesome task of raising babies to become mature adults. Because Betty Friedan craved validation, she was unable to give freely without expecting or needing something in return. She couldn't understand how other women, other *people*, could get satisfaction from sacrifice.

Rather than get the personal help she needed, Friedan concluded that American women live in a patriarchy. Women aren't men's equals, she said. Men get to go out and lead independent lives while women are stuck at home with the kids. That men's lives can be just as unfulfilling or stressful (though in a different way) was never entertained. According to Friedan, there's only one reason for "the problem that has no name": women are oppressed. The way to remedy this injustice, she said, is for women to forgo taking care of their children altogether and pursue fulfilling careers. In short, *The Feminine Mystique* offered American women an out—out of their maternal responsibilities.

Since the feminist movement first took hold in America, the social expectations of women have changed dramatically. Women who have absorbed Friedan's message, either consciously or subconsciously, no longer feel morally obligated to care for their own children. As John Malkovich's character in *The Changeling* says, "Once you give people the freedom to do what they want as the Lord found them in the Garden of Eden, they will do exactly that."

Feminists' success in normalizing absentee parenting is evident everywhere. Consider Colleen. She is a mother of six, whose children (at the time) ranged in age from three months to twelve years. When she went to a chiropractor to get help with her back, the doctor—who was male—asked Colleen about her family life. When she told him she had six children, he asked, "Where do they go during the day?" Colleen told him the name of the school her older children attended, but it was summer at the time, so the doctor asked, "Do you use the YMCA day care then?" Colleen was bewildered. It seemed obvious to her that any woman who chose to have a large family would be home with them. She told him no.

This scenario could only exist in a country that has fully absorbed leftist ideology. To *assume* that mothers no longer care for their own children is astounding. No self-respecting conservative should even try to identify with feminism.

In May 2009, Larry King spent an hour on the subject of "women and self-worth." His guests were, naturally, five feminists who didn't call themselves feminists: actress Della Reese, journalist Lisa Ling, author Lisa Nichols, Martha Stewart, and psychologist Cheryl Saban, who had just written the book called *What Is Your Self-Worth? A Woman's Guide to Validation.* (The word *validation* is key. Thirty years after Friedan exposed her own weakness, the need for validation remains a key feminist trait.)

In her book, Saban wrote, "My goal is to put women's expression of self-worth on the front burner—to put the importance of our validity center stage. . . . Today's young women feel stifled, and in some cases, dominated."[4]

Larry King opened the program by asking the panel, "How does a woman get self-confident?" Della Reese responded, "I suggest you get financially independent, because that gives you freedom and empowerment to love yourself first." (*Empowerment* is another key term feminists use.)

"But haven't things improved with women's rights?" asked King.

"We still need to be defined by a man," Ling responded. "We need to become independent."

Nichols responded with the best line of the program: "Once you are complete, you look for others in your life to complement your completeness."

This exchange is classic feminist tutelage. If you can get past the psychobabble (it's hard, we know), you realize the goal is no different from Friedan's. Feminism is about female empowerment and validation. It's about helping inherently insecure women feel better about themselves. But their proposed solution to this problem—to rearrange society to accommodate women's insecurities—is absurd.

For forty years, women on the left have argued for the same tired notion of female independence—that women should be self-supporting, sexually uninhibited, and liberated from the sacrifices and demands of marriage and motherhood. This still relatively new worldview is more than a fad; it is now firmly established in American culture. The message is played out in the media ad nauseam, and it has produced a generation of young women who are chronically dissatisfied. Modern women are endlessly searching for their identities. They're bored with their sexual freedom (despite their insistence that one-night stands are liberating) and despondent from living a life devoid of commitment. The source of their quandary is that feminists have taught women to abandon the old standards but haven't provided them with any new rules that work!

Another social phenomenon has emerged from feminism: the Mommy Wars. This is the conflict between those who believe mothers should stay at home with their children and those who believe that is too lowbrow a career for intelligent women. Rather than accept parenting as a social responsibility, feminists put motherhood under the umbrella of "a woman's right to choose"—as if raising children is about what women want, rather than what children need. This is a dramatic departure from the cultural ethos of previous generations, in which raising the children one brings into this world was considered a bona fide moral obligation.

There has, fortunately, been a resurgence of at-home motherhood in the past decade; but the cause of the turnaround seems to be in question. Some believe the reason mothers today *can* stay home—other than the fact that they're supposedly wealthy (which is a red herring, as we explain in chapter 5)—is because feminists like Friedan gave choices to women. But Friedan did nothing of the sort. "Many of the welcome changes in women's prospects feminists take credit for were well under way when Betty Friedan was a frustrated housewife seething in the suburbs. In 1963, nearly half of American women worked outside the home, pursuing opportunities all by their helpless selves," wrote Kate O'Beirne.[5]

What Friedan *did* do, like all feminists do, is turn her personal problems outward and blame society. As a result, American women began to believe they really are oppressed.

But there are two main problems with Friedan's theory.

First, it just isn't true that American women in the 1950s were oppressed. Oppression is defined as "the exercise of authority or power in a burdensome, cruel, or unjust manner." The idea that there was a structure in place in America that systematically held women down—such as Sharia law in some countries that forces women to wear a burqa or work only certain jobs—is absurd. Thousands of women in America worked outside the home in various capacities long before feminism came along (even before the World War II era). The only reason modern women don't know this is because their mothers, their college professors, and their female bosses—along with the women in the media—paint a false picture of women in America, one that dismisses the stories of successful women who do not fit the feminist mold.

Take, for example, Carolyn Graglia. She graduated from the same law school as Justice Ruth Bader Ginsburg, several years earlier. Justice Ginsburg has been carrying the feminist torch for decades, making the argument that women in her day were treated as second-class citizens and had to break through the "glass ceiling" (an architectural fiction that Carly Fiorina demolished as CEO of Hewlett-Packard.

But Graglia said that her experience proves otherwise. "From the time I was in junior high school when I decided to become a lawyer until I ceased working in order to raise a family, I received unstinting encouragement and support. Teachers and counselors in high school and college energetically assisted in my efforts without ever questioning the suitability of my aspirations."[6]

Graglia also wrote that her female friends who chose to be housewives and mothers in no way resembled the caricature Friedan presented in *The Feminine Mystique*. These women were perfectly content with their lives at home, and did not feel as if they had "no other option" besides motherhood.

"Workplace discrimination played no part in the decisions many of us made to cease working outside the home. We were impelled to stay with our children by the strong emotional pull they exercised on us and because we thought our presence was the single best guarantee of their well-being."[7] This is a salient observation even today, as it gets to the heart of the "working mom" guilt we hear so much about (which we discuss at length in Chapter 5).

Some may be tempted to say that's just the experience of one woman. But it's not. It is the experience of one woman *who took the time to write about it.* There are plenty of other Carolyn Graglias—like Phyllis for example, whose career spans five decades, or Suzanne's mother, who had a twenty-year career selling stocks that began in the 1950s. In a *St. Louis Post-Dispatch* news article (circa 1966), under the heading "Today's Women," Suzanne's mother said, "When I entered the investment field in St. Louis eleven years ago, there were only three women stockbrokers. Today there are about twenty."[8] The article says Suzanne's mother's "fidelity" to her job is evident by the fact that she was "deep in stocks and bonds on May 14 and gave birth to her daughter on May 15. After a summer of part-time investment counseling, she intends to return to the office full time in September."[9] Sounds awfully similar to the articles we read today.

Yet how was this possible if women in those days were so oppressed?

Another example is Midge Decter. At eighty-three, her experience in the 1950s also differs sharply from the stories feminists tell. Decter had no problem finding employment as a young woman: she first worked as an editor, and later at CBS Records, and then at *Harper* magazine. Like Graglia, Decter's memory of her years at home bears no resemblance to Friedan's version. "I happened to know a lot of women, and they didn't seem either depressed or oppressed to me. Some went back to work when their children were old enough; some became active in local civic organizations; and some got interested in politics. Living in the suburbs was the result of a *decision,* rather than the imposition of a sexist society."[10]

The second problem with Friedan's theory is that her argument that American housewives were bored is misleading. A woman's need for something to do or think about other than caring for her children has nothing to do with the times or culture in which she lives. Her reaction to motherhood is based on her personality. Anyone can be bored or unfulfilled at virtually any job. How one chooses to respond to boredom is key. Most women are resourceful: when faced with boredom, they find a way out. That's an essential skill. Those who don't have it will suffer, to be sure, but that is not society's problem.

Nevertheless, feminists have been successful in getting the majority of Americans to believe that millions of women in the 1950s all realized simultaneously that they were "entitled" to a life outside the home and then expressed this desire only to encounter discrimination at every turn. What was really happening was that technological advances were producing so many labor-saving devices, such as dishwashers and dryers, that women didn't have to spend as much time on household chores. They were thus able to turn their attention elsewhere. Once women realized they had more free time, things began to change naturally. Women began entering the workforce—and they did so *without* feminism.

None of this is to suggest that women in the 1950s never experienced discrimination, but whatever sexism they did encounter wasn't a result of a patriarchal conspiracy designed to keep women in their place. Surely some men were like this, but most were not. (Men are really much nicer than feminists want us to believe.) Moreover, the idea that the average

1950s housewife was despondent and/or subservient to her husband—as Hollywood loves to portray in movies like *Far From Heaven, The Hours,* and *Revolutionary Road*—is a feminist myth. The only reason people consider this a fact is that those who *were* despondent—feminists—spoke the loudest and carried on the most. Had they been stronger women, they could have handled their circumstances differently.

What many Americans don't appreciate is that back in the 1950s, for every one unhappy mom, there were probably a hundred happy moms. Some were content to be homemakers, and some—without attacking society—found their way outside the confines of the home. Feminists were not capable of doing this.

Indeed, most of the prominent feminists were ill equipped to handle adversity. Virginia Woolf, for example, was plagued by periodic mood swings and emotional illnesses. Her mother died suddenly when Woolf was thirteen, and her sister died two years later. These events led to the first of several of Woolf's breakdowns, and it was later revealed that she had been sexually abused by her half brothers. At age fifty-nine, Woolf committed suicide.

Betty Friedan was also afflicted with family problems. She wrote in her autobiography, *Life So Far,* that no matter what she did, her mother made her feel "messy, clumsy, inadequate, bad, naughty, ugly." Friedan spent years in psychoanalysis "talking endlessly about how I hated my mother and how she had killed my father." "All mothers should be drowned at birth," she used to say.[11]

Gloria Steinem is yet another example. Her mother spent long periods in and out of sanatoriums for the mentally disabled. She had a nervous breakdown that left her an invalid, trapped in delusional fantasies that occasionally turned violent. Steinem was only ten years old when her parents finally divorced in 1944, and Steinem spent six years living with her mother in a rundown home in Toledo, Ohio, before leaving for college. When asked about her feelings toward marriage and motherhood, she told *People* magazine, "I'd already been the very small parent of a very big child—my mother. I didn't want to end up taking care of someone else (Biography.com, 2010 A&E Televevision Networks)."

The list goes on. Simone de Beauvoir was a spoiled child who used tantrums to get her way—her sister was apparently her only friend. And Beauvoir's father had indicated that he had always wanted—but never got—a son.

It is very sad that these women had painful upbringings and were haunted by them throughout their lives—we do not mean to minimize it. But that doesn't mean—*it can't mean*—that society should be turned upside down to accommodate their pain. Nor does it change the fact that millions of other women in America overcame their personal problems and lived good lives. *They* are the women we should be hearing from in the media.

The popular phrase, "The personal is political," was coined in the 1960s and refers to making women's personal problems societal problems, and then a matter of public policy. Betty Friedan even admits it! "I almost lost my self-respect trying to hold on to a marriage that was based no longer on love but on dependent hate. It was easier for me to start the women's movement than to change my own personal life."[12]

That is serious perspective.

Nevertheless, the success of Friedan's book took on a life of its own. The media, always a liberal bunch, joined the feminist movement in spades—and encouraged Americans to do likewise. The feminists' first major battle was the Equal Rights Amendment, and it provides an excellent glimpse into the strategy, tactics, and objectives of the female left—as well as its political and media power.

BEHIND THE SCENES OF ERA

The Equal Rights Amendment (ERA), the favorite feminist legislative goal, was a proposed amendment to the United States Constitution, advertised as a great benefit to women—something that would rescue them from centuries of second-class citizenship and for the first time put women in the Constitution. Feminists convinced millions of Americans that women are discriminated against by a male-dominated social and legal structure, and thus the Constitution should be changed to prohibit any difference of treatment based on "sex."

ERA was passionately debated across America from 1972 to 1982. Passing Congress with only 23 out of 435 representatives and only 8 out of 100 senators voting no, ERA was sent to the states on March 22, 1972. Feminists had the semantics, the media, and the momentum on their side. The Equal Rights Amendment sounds so benign, who could possibly oppose it? Within the first twelve months, it was ratified in thirty states and needed only eight more states to become the Twenty-seventh Amendment to the Constitution. Supporting ERA were all those who had pretensions to political power from left to right, from Ted Kennedy to George Wallace, and three presidents: Richard Nixon, Gerald Ford, and Jimmy Carter.

Only one lone senator out of a hundred was willing to speak out against ERA—senator Sam Ervin—and a mere three House members out of 435: Henry Hyde, George Hansen, and Bob Dornan. ERA was actively supported by prominent women's organizations, a consortium of thirty-three women's magazines, numerous Hollywood and television celebrities (such as Phil Donahue, who called himself a feminist and was, at the time, bigger on TV than Oprah), and 99 percent of the media.

But a little band of unflappable ladies in red, wearing Stop ERA buttons, headquartered in Phyllis Schlafly's kitchen on the bluffs of the Mississippi River in Alton, Illinois, challenged all the big guns of modern politics—much like today's Tea Partiers. However, there was no Rush Limbaugh warning about "feminazis," and no Fox News to give fair and balanced news and let the audience decide. The Stop ERA ladies didn't even have the support of conservative magazines because conventional wisdom said their task was impossible. Stop ERAers had no Internet, no e-mail, and no fax machines to rally support for their cause. They had only the telephone and the *Phyllis Schlafly Report*, a four-page monthly newsletter that started their apparently hopeless campaign with its February 1972 issue called "What's Wrong with 'Equal Rights' for Women?"

Over the ten-year period, Phyllis wrote a hundred issues of her monthly newsletter and flyers about ERA. Her reports defined the legal rights women would lose if ERA were ever ratified. They showed that ERA was a fraud. While pretending to benefit women, ERA would actually eliminate rights that women then possessed, such as the right of an eighteen-year-old girl not to be drafted and sent into military combat and the right of a wife to be supported by her husband.

The Stop ERAers got their ammunition straight from the writings of the pro-ERA legal authorities, such as ACLU lawyer Ruth Bader Ginsburg's book *Sex Bias in the U.S. Code*[13] and Yale professor Thomas I. Emerson's lengthy analysis in the *Yale Law Journal*.[14] The military draft proved to be a major argument because the United States was just coming out of the Vietnam War. Most pro-ERAers were over draft age and enthusiastically confirmed that they wanted to make the military draft sex neutral and send girls to war just like men.

Stop ERAers argued that ERA would give a blank check to the federal courts to define the words *sex* and *equality of rights*.

Section 2 of ERA would transfer to the federal government power over all laws that traditionally allowed differences of treatment on account of sex: marriage, property, divorce, alimony, child custody, adoptions, abortion, homosexual laws, sex crimes, private and public schools, prison regulations, and insurance. To feminists, "sex equality" included same-sex marriage and the right to abortion funding. ERA did not mention women—it called for "equality . . . on account of sex." Yet all reporters consistently called ERA the "equal rights *for women* amendment."

In the media, the pro-ERAers peddled the notion that ERA would give women better jobs and a pay raise. Stop ERAers exposed that as fraudulent because U.S. employment laws had already been made sex-neutral (without any help from feminists) before ERA was voted out of Congress. The ERAers claimed their amendment would "put women in the Constitution," but the Stop ERAers actually read the Constitution. They explained how the Constitution is already sex-neutral, using gender-neutral words such as "*we* the people," *person, citizen, resident, author, President, Senator,* and *Member.* In order to make sure Americans understood both sides of the issue, Stop ERAers distributed a booklet published by the National Organization for Women (NOW) called *Revolution: Tomorrow Is NOW,* which set forth NOW's radical feminist, pro-abortion, and anti-Christian agenda.

Throughout the 1970s, the women's liberation movement— led by Steinem and Friedan—enjoyed unparalleled access to the media. Feminists put Phyllis up against all their heavyweights, starting with Betty Friedan in 1973 at Illinois State University, where Friedan famously said to Phyllis, "I'd like to burn you at the stake."

The only forum where Stop ERA received equal time with feminists was at the state legislative hearings. Stop ERAers presented legislators with powerful arguments and documentation provided by the *Phyllis Schlafly Report*. Phyllis made forty-one treks to state capitols (some several times): including those in Little Rock, Richmond, Jefferson City, Atlanta, Raleigh, Phoenix, Columbia, Springfield, Charleston, Nashville, Tallahassee, Augusta, Montpelier, Providence, Denver, Frankfort, Austin, Pierre, Bismarck, Carson City, Dover, Boise, Indianapolis, Topeka, Lincoln, Columbus, and Salt Lake City. In 1976, Stop ERA ladies picketed the White House to protest Betty Ford's lobbying for ERA and again in 1977 to protest Rosalynn Carter's lobbying for ERA.

Springfield, Illinois, where the legislature voted down ERA every year for ten years, was ground zero in the battle. Stop ERA staged many demonstrations, attracting thousands of citizens opposed to the amendment. Media and political pressures in favor of the amendment were so powerful and persistent that nobody believed ERA could be defeated. Legislators were intimidated by the constant drumbeat of the media, the razzmatazz of personal lobbying by Hollywood and television celebrities such as Alan Alda and Marlo Thomas, big money, and pushy feminists.

The tide turned on April 27, 1976, when a thousand people came to Springfield to oppose ERA. That's the day the pro-family movement was invented. People of all religious denominations and walks of life came into the political process for the first time and began to work together for a common political goal—namely, protection of the family and of the Constitution itself against radical feminists.

When ERA was voted out of Congress in 1972, it was given a specific deadline of seven years. When the ERAers realized they were running out of time—and arguments—Congress appropriated the then significant sum of $5 million to stage a tax-funded feminist convention in Houston under the chairmanship of the aggressive New York feminist, Congresswoman

Bella Abzug. Called International Women's Year (IWY), it was designed as a massive media event to persuade the remaining states to ratify ERA. When it opened in Houston, three first ladies were sitting on the platform: Rosalynn Carter, Betty Ford, and Lady Bird Johnson. Among the delegates was every feminist you ever heard of, along with many elected officials. Three thousand members of the media came to give 24/7 press and television coverage.

Feminists cheered for ERA, and then rallied behind their other demands: taxpayer funding of abortions, the entire gay rights agenda, universal day care, and some twenty other feminist goals. After they released their balloons and pranced around with their placards, the whole country realized *why* they were pushing so hard for ERA—and what kind of women were pushing. The most popular buttons worn by delegates were, "A woman without a man is like a fish without a bicycle" and, "Mother Nature is a lesbian." At various booths, you could pick up booklets on "What Lesbians Do." The tremendous media coverage backfired, for it showed Americans what feminism is really about. Since International Women's Year, ERA has been voted on about twenty-five times—in state legislatures, in Congress, and in several statewide referenda. But it never scored another victory.

Since IWY turned out to be a public relations disaster, President Jimmy Carter and Congress gave the ERAers a three-year time extension (later held unconstitutional by a federal court). Political cartoonists had a field day. One cartoon pictured the extension as giving three more innings to a baseball game that was not tied up. The time extension increased the intensity and nastiness of the battle. Excommunicated Mormon Sonja Johnson staged a hunger strike in the rotunda of the Illinois state capitol. She was joined by Dick Gregory and other experienced anti–Vietnam War hunger strikers. A group of pro-ERAers chained themselves to the door of the senate chamber. On June 25, 1982, ERA supporters went to the local slaughterhouse, bought plastic bags of pigs' blood, and used it to write on the Illinois capitol's marble floor the names of the legislators they hated the most. Fortunately, those tactics were unpersuasive.

Time was running out for ERA, but ERAers never ran out of money. In the last weeks before their second deadline, they spent $15 million on a television advertising campaign featuring Hollywood celebrities such as Ed Asner ("Lou Grant") and Carroll O'Connor ("Archie Bunker"). The most dramatic Illinois vote came on June 18, 1980. Tension was high, and all the national media were in the house gallery. President Jimmy Carter telephoned Democratic legislators and promised them federal housing projects in their districts if they would vote yes on ERA. Governor James Thompson telephoned Republican legislators and promised "dams, roads and bridges" in their districts for a yes vote. Mayor Jane Byrne phoned Chicago legislators and threatened that they and their relatives would be fired from their city patronage jobs unless they voted yes. Democratic legislators who were beholden to the Chicago machine wept publicly as they apologized for having to vote yes so their relatives wouldn't lose their jobs. Cash bribes flowed, and the media were gloating.

But Illinois again voted no. On June 4, 1982, when North Carolina defeated ERA for the last time, pro-ERAers sent bags of chicken manure to the twenty-three senators who voted no. And on June 21, Florida defeated ERA for the last time. ERA died when the unconstitutional time extension expired at midnight on June 30, 1982.

The end of ERA was certainly not the end of feminism. On the contrary, the movement is still going strong. "What feminists failed to achieve in that one fell, ill-considered legislative swoop was downright modest compared to their later success in reshaping every facet of American life," wrote O'Beirne.[15] Indeed, feminists set out to "fundamentally transform the United States" decades long before Barack Obama articulated that as his presidential goal.

FIGHTING HUMAN NATURE

Now that we know about ERA and some of the movement's ringleaders, it is important to understand the goals of the female left—for they are no less ambitious today. Three overarching tenets of the feminist movement have become infused in our society. The first we've already addressed: *Feminists are imprisoned by their negative view of women and their place in the world around them.* This view was best expressed in an advertisement by the National Organization of Women (NOW) that was run in many magazines and newspapers during the 1970s. It showed a darling, curly-headed girl over the caption, "This normal, healthy baby has a handicap. She was born female."

This is the basic, chip-on-the-shoulder tenet of feminism that says someone—it is not clear who, perhaps God, perhaps the Establishment, perhaps a conspiracy of male chauvinist pigs— dealt women a foul blow by making them female. Thus, women must hurl demands on society in order to wrest from a male-dominated social structure the status that has been wrongfully denied to women throughout the centuries. Feminists achieve this goal by generating conflicts—in legislatures, in courts, in schools, in universities, and in the workplace (the focus of chapters 6 and 7)—which we are still dealing with today.

The second tenet of feminism is that, *of all the injustices perpetuated on women through the centuries, the most oppressive is that women have babies and men do not.* The abolition of this inequality is the primary goal. That is why women on the left are compulsively driven to make abortion and day care universally available to all women—and taxpayer funded. Women on the left believe they can achieve equality with men only if they can control the number of babies they have (through contraception and abortion) and can outsource (through nannies or day care) the care of the babies they do have. Eliminate the babies, and the equality goal will be achieved.

The third tenet of feminism is that *there is no difference between males and females other than their sex organs.* All those physical, cognitive, and emotional differences you *think* exist are merely social constructs, the result of centuries of restraints and stereotypes imposed by a male-dominated society. That is why feminists become defensive when new research is published that proves innate differences between men and women. It is also why they try to stop grants to scholars who might uncover evidence of differences. Feminists get upset at any argument that shows men and women are not interchangeable. Proof of innate differences interferes with their hope of creating a new society.

For example, in a recent interview, Gloria Steinem was asked about her thoughts on the latest research on male and female brains, which shows a clear and undeniable distinction between males and females. Steinem's response? "Well, you know, every time there is a step forward, there's a backlash. So now we're seeing another backlash about brains, brain differences, gender differences centered in the brain. Even if they're right, it doesn't have to continue to be so. What makes human beings the species that has survived all this time is our adaptability."[16] When the interviewer pressed further and asked, "But aren't there inherent differences we can't ignore?" Steinem replied, "Society can certainly intervene at a cultural level to change that behavior."[17]

Denial is a feminist's ultimate argument. You'd think by now these women would accept that gender differences are real, but they haven't—and they never will. In her 2010 book, *The Male Brain*, Dr. Louann Brizendine explains the latest research that shows how the male brain differs from the female brain. (She also wrote an earlier book called *The Female Brain*.) "The behavioral influences of male and female hormones on the brain are major. My son didn't turn Barbie into a sword because his environment promoted the use of weapons. He was practicing the instincts of his male brain to aggressively protect and defend."[18]

Another example of male nature can be summed up in one woman's description of her husband, Paul, and their two sons, David and Craig: "I'll never understand why David and Craig think passing gas is so funny. But they think it's hilarious, and Paul laughs as hard as *they* do."[19] Can you imagine a husband saying this same thing about his wife and daughters?

Consider the sexual differences between men and women. How many young men do you know who would be offended if a woman told him she'd like to use his body for sex? As George Gilder wrote in *Men and Marriage*, "Young men are subject to nearly unremitting sexual desires, involving their very identity as males. Unless they have an enduring relationship with a woman, men will accept almost any convenient sexual offer."[20] Now turn this scenario around. If a man told *a woman* he'd like to use her body for sex, it would be grounds for sexual harassment.

Apples and oranges.

The truth is, gender differences are the most natural thing in the world—and smart Americans embrace them rather than fight them. Accepting that men and women are different doesn't mean women cannot be doctors or engineers or that men can't be full-time dads—nor does it mean that all men and all women have identical sexual drives. It just means that more men than women may like engineering, more women than men may want to stay home with the kids, and more men than women have a stronger sex drive.

That women *want* to raise their own children rather than outsource this work to hired help is feminists' main bone of contention with American women. Feminists don't want women to want to be with their children; it messes up their plan to change society. In 1976, the French feminist (and Marxist) icon Simone de Beauvoir was so bold as to say that "no woman should be authorized to stay home to raise her children. Women should not have that choice, because if there is such a choice, too many women will make that one."[21]

Don't think this mind-set no longer exists. Just a few years ago, Linda Hirshman, retired professor of philosophy and women's studies at Brandeis University, said, "I think it's a mistake for these highly educated and capable women to make that choice [to stay home]. An educated, competent adult's place is in the office."[22]

WORKPLACE DISCRIMINATION

One of the ways feminists try to appeal to American women is by insisting they're discriminated against in the workplace. To drive home the point, they repeat their mantra that women earn only seventy-seven cents for every dollar men make. "We continue to fight for fairness and equality for America's working women. The Lilly Ledbetter law gives women the tools to fight pay discrimination in the workplace. But we still have not achieved equal pay," said Speaker of the House Nancy Pelosi.

What bunk.

To begin with, if women today *are* discriminated against,

the Equal Employment Opportunity Commission (EEOC), an aggressive federal agency, will take their case. Second, and more important, there is a perfectly good explanation for why women don't make as much money as men: most women do not have the desire to live the life required for most high-pay positions.

No man or woman rises to high-income ranks on a forty-hour week. Ask any successful doctor, lawyer, or business executive. They have spent years working nights and weekends, bringing home briefcases bulging with work and serving clients or customers in a steady stream outside of office hours. These folks have paid a big price for their career and financial success. For any man or woman who chooses that life, there is plenty of room at the top.

There are fewer female politicians for the same reason. In March 2010, *More* magazine featured the lives of three female U.S. representatives (all Democrats, of course—most women who are hailed as role models in the media usually are) in an article called "The Girls in the House." Their story is a feminist's dream: Unlike 99 percent of women in America, Carolyn Maloney, sixty-nine; Debbie Wasserman Schultz, forty-three; and Melissa Bean, forty-eight—*all mothers* (Maloney's children are adults)—take refuge in one another from their exhausting days on Capitol Hill. The three women live together, while their husbands hold down the couples' respective forts in New York, Florida, and Illinois.

Clearly, most women would not choose to leave their husbands and children behind and move to another city to live with other women and devote their lives to their jobs. Even if their families moved to Washington with them, a life in politics is no easy life. "Your D.C. days often start with predawn workouts, sunrise media events or breakfast meetings, and may not end until final votes are cast at 10 or 11 at night," wrote Annie

Groer in the *More* article. Congresswoman Bean admits, "Members of Congress almost never have dinner with their families."[23]

Missing from the article was the truth about how hard this life is on women and their families. Instead, their lives are treated as normal, even admirable. Remember: Elite feminists pretend they are just like everyone else. "Like all women in America, we are trying to juggle our public and our private lives, the difficulty of getting home for a child's doctor appointment or school play, the balance between work and family," says Maloney.[24]

Feminists are delusional—Ms. Maloney and her cohorts are *not* "like all women in America." Most women have no desire to do the work necessary to win elections—drive thousands of miles, shake hundreds of strangers' hands, eat third-rate chicken suppers, and attend political meetings every night and weekend. And most women certainly don't want to subject themselves to political attacks that impugn their integrity and probe into their personal lives and finances. Much to feminists' dismay, most women with children—if they work outside the home at all—work part-time. And they like it that way. Their lives bear no resemblance to the lives of congresswomen, or doctors, or lawyers, or CEOs.

LIVING IN THE WAKE OF FEMINISM

Americans are badly mistaken if they think feminism is dead. "Younger women argue that by accepting [feminism] as natural, they are paying tribute to their predecessors," wrote Susan Toepfer in the *Wall Street Journal* blog.[25] There you have it: feminism is "natural." While surveys show that young women don't want to be called feminists, that's only because they don't want to be aligned with fringe feminists. Most modern women, regardless of how they vote, fully accept and embrace what they *think* is the basic tenet of feminism: equality for women. They genuinely believe they owe the "sisterhood" a debt of gratitude. Feminism isn't dead—it's *in the air.*

Even worse, it is now part of the larger Democratic agenda. In *Political Emancipation,* author Andre Harper wrote about how blacks in America have endured leftist indoctrination for years. His story could be any white American woman's story—just substitute "sexist" for "racist," and "woman" for "black man."

As a black man, Harper was raised to believe America was an inherently racist country in which black people were held back by "mean" Republicans who don't want to see blacks succeed. As Harper grew older and began thinking for himself, he realized the opposite is true. He learned that Democrats project care and concern, but in fact they create policies designed to keep black people from succeeding and dependent on government. As long as there's an underclass, Harper realized, Democrats can create more government jobs. Remove the underclass, and Democrats have no one to fight for. "As a young black man, I realized early on that there was a stigma attached to me that was created by liberals in order to make the case for why they then need to advocate on my behalf and get more program dollars to provide for me. Liberals want you to believe [blacks] are born at a deficit."[26]

Harper's analysis of the Democratic Party is spot-on, and the *female* Democratic agenda is no different. Feminists are financially and politically invested in getting American women to believe they are born at a deficit and thus need feminists to advocate on their behalf. (*The Shriver Report* is a terrific example.) As long as women choose to be wives and mothers, as they traditionally have, left-wing women have no mission. That's why they push the notion that traditional America is obsolete and that everyone should accept it as fact. As *The*

Shriver Report gloats, "Mothers are the primary breadwinner or co-breadwinner in two-thirds of American families. Three-quarters of Americans view this as a positive development for society."[27]

This is total myth. According to Public Agenda, the premier nonpartisan polling agency in New York, 70 percent of parents with children under age five agree that "having a parent at home is best," and a full 72 percent of parents—including the majority of low-income parents!—believe *parents*, not the government, are responsible for child care costs. Moreover, 63 percent of parents of children under five *disagree* with the idea that children in day care receive "just as good" care and attention as with a stay-at-home parent. It is also worth noting that six in ten Americans rate their generation as only "fair" or "poor" in raising children.[28]

Shriver's claim that "three-quarters of Americans view [two-income families] as a positive development for society" is simply not true. What she's referring to is that Americans have no qualms about mothers working outside the home *in general.* That's not the same thing as being an advocate for absentee parenting. Once again, feminists manipulate facts to suggest something entirely different from their actual meaning.

One of the ways 1970s feminists lured women out of the home was to demand that they focus their education on subjects that would advance their careers, rather than focus on subjects related to homemaking or teaching. Elite feminists push all women to plan their lives around careers. The result is that young women give little thought to marriage and motherhood and instead spend upwards of a decade becoming highly qualified for the workforce. Women believe this is the better life plan, since their mothers' lives, they are told, were empty and meaningless. Women in previous decades may have had jobs, but they didn't have *careers.* Like tempting children with candy, feminists assured women there was a better life to be had. "Whether girls heard the call of independence from their family or the outside culture, they listened," wrote Dr. Jean Twenge in *Generation Me*.[29]

For centuries, women considered marriage and motherhood to be their highest calling and planned their lives accordingly, and many of those who didn't regretted it. Countless celebrities— Joanne Woodward, Barbara Walters, Jamie Lee Curtis, to name a few—have warned women there are trade-offs if women try to have family and career all at once. Some even said that if they could do it all over again, they would have stayed home with their children when they were young.

A major difference between today's generation and previous generations is that in the past, society respected motherhood and all that it entails. Those who didn't choose to make the sacrifice admitted that they couldn't successfully juggle family and career. Asked why she never had children, Katharine Hepburn said, "Well, I'm not dumb enough to think I could have handled that situation. If your mind is on something else, you are useless. If someone needs you, they need YOU! That's why I think women have to choose. I remember making the decision, 'Well, I'll never marry and have children. I want to be a star, and I don't want to make my husband and children my victims.'"[30] Oprah Winfrey has made similar claims.

This is *not* the attitude of the average young woman, who has been raised under the slogan of "choice." Her life is about her, and her alone. That's why her plans look different from the plans of women in previous generations. If asked, she'll tell you the reason she plans her life the way she does is because women in America have made so much progress, or that a good standard of living requires two incomes.

Let's take a look at the modern woman's plans, and you can determine for yourself if it looks like progress.

Anna is twenty-nine. She has been in school for more than ten years. First she gets a bachelor's degree, then a master's, then a Ph.D. Throughout this time, Anna lives with her boyfriend, Sam. Sam has finished medical school and does his residency in the same state where Anna is in school. Things are going well for both of them, and soon they become engaged.

By the time Anna gets her Ph.D. and Sam completes his residency, they are both thirty-one years old and newly married. They need to find jobs and are concerned about whose job should take precedence. In the midst of their quandary, Anna discovers she's pregnant, and Sam is offered a job as a family practitioner in another state, far away from both of their families. He takes the job, not because it's the one he really wanted but because Anna is pregnant and the pressure to provide for a family is on.

Toward the end of Anna's pregnancy, she finds a job in their new city and quickly begins her search for child care. She finds the perfect nanny—or so she thinks. After several months, she learns her perfect nanny isn't so perfect. She finds a new nanny who doesn't work out either. After three nannies, she gives up and puts the baby in day care.

After a year or so, Anna struggles unsuccessfully to get pregnant again because of her age. She resorts to in vitro fertilization. The process is long and painful, but eventually she conceives, and two years later another baby is born. Anna soon discovers the demands of a toddler and baby to be overwhelming—particularly since Grandma is not around to help. She decides she doesn't want to return to work because it's all too much—so she quits, which is just as well because, as it turns out, Anna enjoys being with her children.

Sam is resentful. Not only do they have enormous debt from Anna's years in school, but Sam planned his career around Anna's career. He doesn't want her to quit her job and has no qualms about putting his children in day care because everyone he knows does the same thing.

Conflict ensues, and the end of their story is anyone's guess.

Stories like these abound. For the past several decades, American women have been pushed to work outside the home—where it is assumed their brains will atrophy from lack of use. Rather than expand their horizons beyond home-making, modern women have done a 180 and seek *the highest possible career aspirations.* Today, women earn 57 percent of college degrees in America—and almost half of the degrees in law and medicine. But to what end? While careers are fulfilling, they do not replace the fulfillment most women get from being wives and mothers. Moreover, these types of careers will inevitably conflict with the demands of home and children. Careers should be icing on the cake—not the cake itself.

Despite the evidence that feminism has been a failure, women still think they identify with its basic premise. Even *conservative* women believe the mass exodus of mothers from the home has been the "consequence of the great feminist revolution that stormed the barricades of the patriarchy and won a glorious victory."[31]

This never happened.

The most important factor that influenced the significant shift of American women into the workplace is the invention of laborsaving devices. The folks to whom women are truly indebted are inventors Thomas Edison (electric lights), Elias Howe (the sewing machine), Clarence Birdseye (the process for frozen foods), and Henry Ford (the automobile). Technology and the mechanization of housework—such as the washing machine, dryer, dishwasher, and vacuum cleaner—allowed women to turn their attention away from household duties.

The birth control pill was another major factor. Americans love to associate "the Pill" with feminism; but it, along with machines of convenience, was invented *before* the 1960s—by *men.* It was the contributions of men that gave women the time to work outside the home in record numbers. Women should be thanking "the men who came before us"—not feminists.

Moreover, the Great Depression forced women to seek employment when the men in their families could not get jobs. During World War II, women in large numbers began to fill jobs for which men were unavailable. The Equal Pay Act of 1963 was also helpful. It abolished wage disparity based on sex. None of these factors—America's inventors, the Great Depression, World War II, and the Equal Pay Act—have anything to do with feminism. Dinesh D'Souza, the conservative author and president of King's College in New York City, called the notion that feminism is responsible for the freedoms women have today "a lovely fairy tale."[32]

The truth is that feminism has been the single worst thing that has happened to American women. It did not liberate women at all—it confused them. It made their lives harder. Women today are caught between man and nature. (It should surprise no one that the most popular bumper sticker used by the women who battled against the Equal Rights Amendment was "You can't fool Mother Nature.") Their female nature tells them sex requires love; marriage is important; children are a blessing; and men are necessary. The culture, meanwhile, tells them to sleep around and postpone family life because that will cost them their identity. And, if their marriage doesn't work out, it's no big deal. They can always get divorced.

Is it any wonder modern women are unhappy?

To answer this question, we must deal with feminists who insist there's no connection between feminism and women's discontent. In April 2010, the *Wall Street Journal* asked the question, "Did Feminism Make Women Miserable?" The reporters consulted—naturally—feminist author Naomi Wolf (who, by the way, is working on a new book called *The Cultural History of the Vagina*—gotta love those feminists!) to help answer the question. Wolf said, "The idea that feminism makes women miserable has been coming up ever since the movement began. It's a perennial because of our deeply held fears that freedom and joy are incompatible."[33] As you can see, the feminist response to any reasonable question is to meander—and end up in a ditch.

As a nation, we cannot keep avoiding the elephant in the room. Feminism has indeed made women miserable. It was a mistake to encourage women to ignore their feminine instincts and whine about how badly they have it. Smart women (aka conservative women) do not need feminism to liberate them from anything. The word *liberation* comes from the word *liberty*, which means "the condition in which an individual has the ability to act according to his or her own will."

Women in America have always had the ability to act according to their own will. It may have been harder several generations ago than it is today—but that's not because women were victims. "It would be hard to find a single example in history in which a group that casts more than 50 percent of the vote got away with calling itself the victim," wrote Warren Farrell, Ph.D., in *The Myth of Male Power*.[34] Women in previous generations simply didn't have the time, or the inclination, to focus so obsessively on their identities.

They also weren't encouraged to sleep around, get divorced, put their children in day care, turn to Uncle Sam as provider, or belittle men. That is strictly leftist territory—and it's been the worst thing that ever happened to this nation.

· 3 ·

HOOK-UPS AND HEARTACHE

The pursuit of promiscuous sexual pleasures leads chiefly
to misery and despair.

—George Gilder

I n the movie *Pleasantville*, a brother and sister from the
1990s are sucked into their television set and find themselves trapped in a 1950s-style television show. Suddenly they
have old-fashioned parents with traditional values. The characters integrate themselves into what they consider a "backward"
society, and they find it difficult. During one conversation
about sex, the daughter (played by Reese Witherspoon) rolls
her eyes at the mother, whom she's convinced knows nothing
about sex. To drive home the point that the 1950s was an era
of sexual repression, the *children* teach the *parents* about sex.

Pleasantville isn't entirely unjustified—today's young people
are more sexually savvy than their parents were. The problem is
the suggestion that earlier generations were trapped and clueless, that they had no idea what they were doing in the bedroom and could have benefited from a little advice. Indeed, the
sexual revolution of the 1960s ushered in a new era in American culture. As feminists began to denigrate the traditional

female role and suggest housewives lacked sexual freedom, the notion of married sex became passé, and free love became the custom of the land. Today, sex is a free-for-all. It no longer carries with it an element of privacy or significance.

The results of this transformation are set forth in Carol Liebau's book *Prude*. Between 1943 and 1999, the age of first intercourse dropped from nineteen to fifteen for females. During the same period, the percentage of sexually active women rose from 13 percent to 47 percent. Between 1969 and 1993, the percentage of female teenagers and young adults having oral sex skyrocketed from 42 percent to 71 percent. But the most dramatic development is young women's beliefs about premarital sex: In 1943, only 12 percent approved of it; by 1999, 73 percent did. That is a dramatic departure from previous cultural mores, and it has had profound consequences—especially for women. "The women who acted upon the teachings of feminist sexual revolutionaries have suffered greatly," wrote Carolyn Graglia in *Domestic Tranquility*.[1]

Miriam Grossman, M.D., a former campus psychiatrist at UCLA and author of the groundbreaking book *Unprotected: A Campus Psychiatrist Reveals How Political Correctness in Her Profession Endangers Every Student,* reports that at the health center where she worked for ten years, almost 70 percent of her patients were women. Dr. Grossman's account of what is happening to our nation's young women is jaw-dropping. "Radical politics pervades my profession, and common sense has vanished."[2]

In the past, she wrote, a campus physician was likely to tell students that marriage was the optimal goal. It was okay to point out that men and women are different, that casual sex is ill advised, and that sexually transmitted diseases are a serious matter to be avoided at all costs. Today, we live in a politically correct culture that rejects such prudent advice.

Planned Parenthood considers promiscuity to be normal, and the pressure on health professionals to share this view is tremendous. Doctors and counselors have been thrust into a world in which they cannot relay certain facts, because to do so would be politically incorrect and would undermine the left-wing agenda.

"Sex education is a social movement. Its goal is to change society. This movement envisions a world without taboos, and without restrictions. It envisions a world free of Judeo-Christian morality. No judging is allowed. In this ideal world, there is complete gender equality. This idea permeates sexual education," says Dr. Grossman. "The problem is that it's not based in reality."[3]

FROM SMART SEX TO CASUAL SEX

Over the past half century, millions of Americans have absorbed the progressive notion that being cavalier with one's body—engaging in the most intimate form of human contact with virtually anyone who crosses our path—is liberating. How did this happen?

At the core of the casual sex phenomenon is the eradication of America's moral order. "Before the sixties, most Americans believed in a universal moral order that is external to us and makes demands on us. Our obligation was to conform to that moral order," wrote Dinesh D'Souza.[4] One of the precepts of this moral order was that sex is an act reserved for marriage. While not everyone managed to wait until they were married to have sex, the goal was a good one—and it was embraced by the majority of Americans. And those who didn't wait for marriage were more likely to be in love with their partner and accept responsibility for their actions.

During the 1960s, however, feminists condemned America's social structure as oppressive and fought for a new worldview— one that didn't involve God or society's rules. Rather, they suggested people should look within themselves to find life's meaning. This philosophy is known as *moral relativity*, a belief that people are to follow their own standards when it comes to making decisions, including decisions about sex. To a moral relativist, being true to oneself is of prime importance. The only criterion is what's right for *you*. "This is the social trend—so strong it's really a revolution: Do what makes you happy."[5]

The rise of moral relativism, along with feminist tutelage, has produced a sea change in sexual morality. Today women who refrain from sexual activity until they are in a committed, monogamous relationship (or even *married*) are viewed with skepticism at best and ridicule at worst. Feminist Jessica Valenti, for example, is an outspoken proponent of hook-ups. In her book, *The Purity Myth*, she makes the argument that women are just like men and, thus, should feel free to sleep around. She uses her own story of losing her virginity as a teenager, suggesting she never understood what all the fuss was about.

In addition to her Web site Feministing, where promiscuous women can find plenty of support for their lifestyle, Valenti speaks on college campuses where she derides conservatives and conservative organizations, such as Miriam Grossman, M.D. Wendy Shalit, Kathleen Parker, Sarah Palin, Fox News, the Independent Women's Forum, and the Clare Boothe Luce Policy Institute.

Feminist author Naomi Wolf is another example. She insists a girl's sex drive is "at least as intense" as a boy's and, like Valenti, encourages women to embrace their inner "slut." These feminists are relics from the 1960s revolution, when sex became a random act. In a documentary titled "Boomer$!" Tom Brokaw interviewed journalist P. J. O'Rourke, who commented on the licentiousness of that generation: "The sexuality was utterly irresponsible, utterly irreligious. We were a bunch of morons."[6]

Indeed, decades of debauchery have resulted in a nation of women prone to sexual disease, unwanted pregnancies, and heartache. In response to this phenomenon, schools have taken on what was once considered the parental domain: teaching young people about sex. But political correctness doesn't allow teachers to make value judgments, so the information America's children receive about sex from a young age is devoid of moral boundaries.

By the time young people go to college, the situation gets worse. Not only do universities up the ante by normalizing any and all sexual behavior, there is zero acknowledgment of self-restraint. The only message young people receive about sex is to "be safe." If they use a condom each time they have sex, they're told, everything will be okay. They can have sex any way they want, with whomever they want, as often as they want. But, alas, everything is not fine—as Dr. Grossman proves in her book *Unprotected*.

Take Olivia, for example, who was one of the hundreds of college students Dr. Grossman counseled at UCLA. Olivia had been valedictorian of her high school senior class and hoped to go to medical school. After she arrived on campus, however, she had a short-term relationship with a young man. After the breakup, Olivia had bouts of bingeing and vomiting and ended up at the campus health center. It seems she had had her first sexual experience with the young man and told Dr. Grossman that she couldn't stop thinking about him. She especially couldn't handle seeing him in class. "Why," Olivia asks, "do they tell you how to protect your body from herpes and pregnancy, but they don't tell you what it does to your *heart*?"[7]

In modern America, we talk a great deal about the obvious consequences of the sexual revolution—sexually transmitted diseases and unintended pregnancies—but another effect has fallen under the radar: women's emotional well-being. For years women have been fed the lie that they're equipped to handle random sex, and many believed it. The result of this pressure is that women engage in hook-ups out of fear that not doing so means there's something wrong with them. Frannie Boyle, a twenty-two-year-old senior at Vanderbilt University, thought hooking up was a way to feel normal and fit in. Fortunately for her, she stopped when she realized it made her feel "so empty."[8]

Psychotherapist and author Kerry Cohen knows this feeling well. In her 2008 memoir, *Loose Girl*, Cohen examines her promiscuous past, which included sleeping with almost forty boys and men. *Loose Girl* is the best evidence to date of how emotionally harmful the sexual revolution has been to women. It is simply impossible to imagine a man authoring this book, which analyzes in detail the emotions that accompany sex. Cohen reviews the reasons why she had sex, why she chose the boys and men she did, how she felt leading up to each encounter, how she felt afterwards, and what she expected to happen compared to what did happen. The bottom line is that Ms. Cohen wanted guys to like her. "I let these men inside me, wanting to make me matter to them."[9]

The average male does not ruminate over who he had sex with or why he did it—he knows why he did it. Nor does he have sex with a woman because he wants her to like him. Men have sex when it's available to them—period. The more offers they get, the better. "For a man, this might be a pleasant trip down memory lane, counting up one's conquests," wrote Cohen. "But for a girl, it's a whole other story."[10]

Women like Boyle and Cohen learned the hard way that hooking up is a dead-end street. For Cohen, it took sleeping with dozens of men before she figured out her behavior was counterproductive. As is often the case, at the heart of Cohen's story is a dysfunctional family. As a child, Cohen's parents divorced, and her father smoked marijuana with his kids. Her mother was emotionally unstable, leaving her children in order to attend medical school in *Milan, Italy* (which Cohen's grandmother called a "strong, brave thing to do"). If Cohen had been raised in an earlier era, or at least by conservative parents, she might have avoided her fate. But everyone to whom she turned for advice over the years supported her lifestyle, including her own mother. Both a pregnancy scare and a bout of genital herpes were treated as lightly as if Cohen had a bad cold.

There are millions of Kerry Cohens in America today—perhaps not *as* promiscuous, but promiscuous nonetheless. They may not all be having sex for the same reasons, but most come away from their sexual encounters the same way Cohen did: they've confused men's interest with love. They thought, or hoped, that if a man was willing to sleep with them, he might be willing to have a relationship, too. In other words, women go against their conscience and have sex first, thinking it will *bring* them love.

One reason women are confused about sex is that they're constantly barraged with politically correct images of men and women hooking up indiscriminately, under the promise that such behavior is empowering to women. They never see the fallout of such behavior. "The characters in *Friends* and *Sex in the City* are not real. In real life, Phoebe would have herpes, and Carrie would have genital warts," wrote Dr. Grossman.[11]

It isn't just professionals who succumb to feminist pressure; parents are expected to do likewise. In the May 2009 issue of *O* magazine, Oprah's favorite sex therapist, Dr. Laura Berman, answers questions about how parents can fight the sex culture to which their daughters are exposed. She offers an example of a new "game" teenagers play called "rainbow parties." Different girls perform oral sex on a boy, and he sees how many colors of lipstick he can collect on his penis by the end of the night. Dr. Berman's suggestion for how parents can talk to their daughters about this activity is to tell them they hope their children understand the risks. She adds that parents should avoid being judgmental or giving their daughters "didactic lectures." Rather, she says, "talk with your daughter about exploring her body or even offer her a simple clitoral vibrator."[12]

This progressive and absurd approach to teenage sexuality misses the point. Girls are not having sex for physical satisfaction. They're having it for one of two reasons: the desire to belong or the desire to be loved. Advice like Dr. Berman's will do nothing to eradicate promiscuity. What *will* help is for women to arm themselves with the kind of education they'll never get in school or in the media. Fortunately, Dr. Grossman, who refers to herself as "100 percent MD, 0 percent PC," has compiled such information. You can find it at the back of this book, in Appendix B.

In the meantime, if we really want to solve this monumental crisis in America, we must first admit where society went wrong.

LIBERAL PARENTING AND THE RISE
OF THE COOL MOM

In reading about our sexualized culture, an obvious question arises: Where on earth are the parents? How did we arrive at a point where the best we can do for our kids is to hand them vibrators and condoms and tell them to have a good time? "Parenting is an incredibly powerful force for spreading cultural values," wrote Dr. Twenge.[13] Indeed it is. Unfortunately, there's been a sea change in parenting over the past few decades.

The modern generation—those in their twenties, thirties, and early forties—has been raised largely by baby boomers.

In keeping with their anti-authority worldview, boomers felt their parents were too strict and decided they were going to do a better job when they had their own kids. Rather than tell their children what to do, boomers were lax in their discipline. They let their kids flounder and figure things out for themselves, rather than saying things like, "This is right, and that is wrong," or, "That is unacceptable behavior," or, "This is a better choice." In other words, they allowed their children to make their own moral decisions long before they had the emotional capacity to do so—which is why so many of them throw caution to the wind.

There's another factor at play. In the liberal mind, an adult—even a *parent*—cannot tell young people what to do if they themselves have engaged in the behavior they're warning against. But this is absurd. "Of all the myths getting in the way of giving better advice to young people, most dangerous is the view that we must be perfect angels in order to have an opinion on anything. But it can't be right that we can never learn from experience, that we must merely clothe, bathe, feed, and shelter our babies, and then tell them, 'Sorry, can't say!' when they ask for our opinions."[14]

One of the results of parents' hands-off approach is promiscuity.

"A new time has come in the history of American girlhood," wrote Caitlin Flanagan in the *Atlantic*.[15] Like Lauren Rhodes, the college student whose mother made her carry a box of condoms, and Kerry Cohen, whose mother treated her pregnancy scare casually, Flanagan's mother told her not to get married just because she wants to have sex. Instead, she said, just have sex.

This attitude is in stark contrast to the World War II era's approach to sex. While it wasn't perfect either, it was sound. It supported the notion that marriage is the ultimate goal and that sex is something to be savored. Taking this approach doesn't mean burying one's head in the sand, as liberals claim. It's just smart.

That's one of the differences between conservative and liberal philosophy. A liberal parent says, "Well, my children are going to do what they want anyway, so I might as well give in and just tell them to be safe." This approach completely misses the point of parenting, which is to give direction to the young. A conservative parent says, "I'm going to explain to my children the pitfalls of casual sex (STDs, unwanted pregnancy, loss of self-respect), instill in them a sense of personal responsibility, let them know how special they and their bodies are, and pray they absorb the message." This approach directs the child to make good and healthy choices.

Conservatives recognize that people will succumb to temptation, but such lapses are not a reason to get rid of standards. This is a concept lost on baby boomers (and leftists). In their attempt to be cool, they dismiss moral standards and harbor an "anything goes" mentality. With boomers, there is no line between child and parent. They treated their children as friends instead of charges, and the result has been disastrous. "It's been almost 50 years since we embarked on an adventure called sex education, all fired up about change and the new world it would bring: open, positive, and free. Where did it get us? From rare instances of teen infections to nine million new cases a year. From two bugs to two dozen. It got us to babies having babies, sixth graders on the pill, teens with cervical cancer, and to HIV and AIDS. Some new world, huh?"[16]

The Counter–Sexual Revolution

The sexual revolution has had a long ride. Fortunately, a counter-revolution is brewing. Numerous studies have shown that when women today go to college, they're marginalized if they don't join the hook-up scene. But girls like Frannie Boyle are tired of being told they have to be cavalier about sex in order to fit in.

Wendy Shalit, author of *A Return to Modesty* and *The Good Girl Revolution*, has spoken with countless young women across the country about their views on sex, dating, and marriage—and roughly 70 percent of her correspondence indicates that women feel they need to hide their desire for marriage and motherhood in order to fit in. Many take part in the casual sex culture just to feel normal. In a study published in the *Archives of Pediatrics and Adolescent Medicine,* 41 percent of girls ages fourteen to seventeen reported having "unwanted sex." This is not to be confused with rape (which a feminist would immediately claim). Instead, the term "unwanted sex" means the girls feel pressured to sleep around. Other studies show that sexually experienced teens, usually girls, wished they had waited longer before having sex.

The pressure to be a good girl was what feminists in the 1960s billed as oppressive, but today the reverse is true. It's oppressive for women to feel they have to be "bad" to fit in—it takes away their dignity, resulting in powerlessness. "Could it be that badness requires more suppression of individual preferences than goodness ever did? The point of delaying gratification was precisely to preserve your individuality, preferences, and goals—and your long-term happiness."[17]

Fortunately, Americans are waking up.

Consider the popular teen film *High School Musical,* which was eerily similar to the 1978 movie *Grease,* except for one thing: it was *more* wholesome. In *Grease*, one of the main characters misses her period after having sex with a boy in the backseat of a car, and a fair portion of the film revolves around the idea that she might be pregnant. In *High School Musical*, the main characters don't even *kiss* until the end of the movie. It's a film that could have easily been made in the 1950s. Yet teens loved it.

They also love the Twilight series and performers like Taylor Swift and the younger Miley Cyrus (not to be confused with the older Miley Cyrus, who ruined her good girl image). And last year, the movie *Flipped*—another wholesome, PG-rated film—was released. It's a coming-of-age romantic comedy that follows a young boy and a young girl as they grow up together in the late '50s and early '60s. These movies and per-formers represent wholesome family entertainment—and kids are smitten. If young girls are telling us anything, it's that they *want* boundaries and standards. They *want* to be reined in. Too much freedom makes children beholden to their physical and emotional desires. It just *feels* wrong.

That's why it's essential for any culture to prescribe norms that facilitate romance and marriage, rather than sexual con-quests. That's what Ms. Shalit tried to do with her first book, *A Return to Modesty*. In it she argues that it's natural for women to be modest and that perhaps we should revisit this notion without deriding women as delusional or repressed for their desire to do so. For taking this position, Shalit's book was deemed controversial. (Kirkus Reviews called it "daring.") That's because the idea that someone, a twenty-three-year-old woman no less, would attempt to resurrect America's "lost virtue" seemed preposterous. Doesn't Shalit know that femi-nists have been fighting for decades to give women the right to do as they please with their bodies? Has the author been living under a rock?

Hardly. The truth is that Shalit is wise beyond her years, and young women would be wise to follow her lead. Women today are no less romantic than they were a hundred years ago. We know this to be true because, despite the enormous opportunities now available to women, they still choose to marry at a young age. More educated women marry slightly later, but not much—*despite* the fact that cohabitation has become socially acceptable, and most women are in the workforce. Women, by nature, don't want cafeteria-style sex. They want to be married.

Unfortunately, thanks to feminists marriage in America is under attack.

· 4 ·

WHY MARRIAGE ELUDES THE
MODERN GENERATION

You become a semi-nonperson when you get married.
—Gloria Steinem

At some point, the free-love culture of today's youth often gives way to marriage, which one might consider a good thing, except for one problem: this generation has no idea *how* to be married, or even how to go about choosing the right spouse.

Two reasons for this phenomenon are often overlooked: (1) men and women have been raised in a culture that refuses to embrace the unique natures of males and females thus their relationships carry unnecessary conflict and strain; (2) most young people have been either directly or indirectly affected by divorce, which has led to a distrust of marriage that, in turn, leads to more divorce. The publishing industry has even developed a genre for this new demographic: the divorce memoir.

Using the written word as a cathartic tool, modern women have been lamenting their divorces, questioning the purpose of marriage, or simply trying to get it right. In the past several years, the books published include: *How Not to Marry the Wrong Guy: Is He "the One" or Should You Run? A Guide to Living Happily Ever After*; *Married to Me: How Committing to Myself Led to Triumph After Divorce*; *A Little Bit Married: How to Know When It's Time to Walk Down the Aisle or Walk Out the Door*; and *Split: A Memoir of Divorce*.

But the most successful of all divorce memoirs is the very popular book (and movie), *Eat, Pray, Love,* in which the author, Elizabeth Gilbert, recounts her painful divorce and personal discovery during a year long romp around the globe. All these books shed light on an extraordinary modern phenomenon: a deep-seated suspicion of marriage as a viable social institution.

How did this happen? For centuries marriage has been considered the bedrock of society—the glue that holds a culture together. The most obvious reason for marriage is to provide a stable environment for children, but there are other advantages. In *The Case for Marriage*, authors Linda Waite and Maggie Gallagher reveal that married people report being happier in general and more satisfied with their sex lives. They earn more, have better physical and mental health, and have better-adjusted children. Surely these are all good reasons to get married and stay married.

More significant, however, is the fact that the overwhelming majority of Americans *want* to be married. Despite the cultural changes we've witnessed over the past half century, the median age of first-time marriages hasn't changed as dramatically as we might expect. In the post–World War II era, men and women married in their early twenties. Today, the median age for first-time marriages is twenty-six for women and twenty-eight for men. Opinion surveys show that marriage and family are still the most important priority for Americans. "Generation X considers being a good wife/mother or husband/father to be the most important sign of success—ahead of money, fame, power, religion, and being true to oneself," wrote Pamela Paul in *The Starter Marriage*.[1]

Clearly, the modern generation has good intentions. Unfortunately, their chances of staying married are bleak, and young people are painfully aware of this fact. In "Couples take their sweet time," *USA Today* writer Sharon Jayson explains that today's young adults are involved in very long relationships prior to getting married, mostly because they're scared.

Their worries are not unfounded. Not only has this generation been raised in a divorce culture, America has changed dramatically. Men's rights have been virtually eliminated (as we discuss in chapter 7), and the emphasis on higher education results in enormous debt owed by young couples. These are hardly ideal circumstances for settling down. Moreover, premarital sex is no longer taboo, which means many couples (about two-thirds) cohabitate instead of getting married. All these developments greatly affect the institution of marriage.

The underlying problem, however, is not with the institution of marriage but with Americans' attitude toward it. If we want to save marriage, we must begin by changing our outlook. How we view something affects the effort we put into it—since this generation struggles with a negative attitude toward marriage, they tend to put less effort into it.

In Jayson's article, people say that they co-habitate in part because they think they can prepare themselves better for marriage and ward off potential disasters. Not only does this convey negativity right off the bat, it's an exercise in futility. There is no way people can know what's going to happen down the line. Cohabitation is not insurance against future doom and gloom—in fact, it *causes* gloom and doom. Couples who live together first (unless they were engaged beforehand) have less chance of marital success than those who did not cohabitate.

But the single greatest obstacle young people face when it comes to marriage is lack of maturity. Unlike previous generations, today's young people have been spoiled. They've grown up with relatively little hardship and few moral demands. "This is the generation that won't commit to going to a party on Saturday because someone better might come along," says psychotherapist Shannon Fox.[2] Moreover, our culture of immediate gratification has not worked in the modern generation's favor. If everything isn't exactly as they want it to be *right now*, they think it will never be. They don't realize their patience will be rewarded down the line. Marriage changes as the years go by—in many cases it gets easier. In fact, studies have shown that couples who once felt dissatisfied in their marriages felt the opposite five years later.

Leaving one relationship for another is no guarantee of a better life, either. A spouse will often pursue a new and exciting relationship in order to escape the problems in the current relationship—only to end up with problems of a different sort in the new relationship. People get caught up in the moment and forget that over time things won't seem so exciting anymore. Infatuations end. As Dr. M. Scott Peck wrote in his wildly successful 1978 book *The Road Less Traveled*, "The feeling of ecstatic lovingness that characterizes the experience of falling in love always passes. The honeymoon always ends. The bloom of romance always fades."[3] Peck explains that romantic love is a myth. Real love involves investing ourselves in the needs and desires of another person. "We must be committed beyond the boundaries of the self."[4]

This is a difficult concept to embrace for a generation that has been raised to value the self above all else. Moreover, movies and television have romanticized marriage beyond reason. Americans are routinely bombarded with the notion that there's one special person "out there" and it's our job to find him or her. But finding someone to marry is a far less romantic task than we wish it were. There are plenty of people in the world with whom we might be well suited, and choosing the right one means being smart as well as romantic.

When, we might ask, did getting married and staying married become so difficult? Not surprisingly, at the same time casual sex became fashionable—the 1960s. That's when feminists began emphasizing the individual over the family good. This shift in focus means American women no longer plan for marriage carefully, methodically, and with foresight. Rather, they are encouraged to focus solely on their identities and their careers. The notion that a woman should follow her own dreams, that she should be true to herself and not be held back by husband and children, has become a fait accompli. Women may want to settle down eventually, but marriage (and motherhood) is something that just sort of happens, as if it were a nice accompaniment to an otherwise fulfilling life. To the modern woman, work is the meat of her life. A husband is the salad.

This is a profound transformation. Married couples no longer think of themselves as one unit but as separate entities sharing space, which leads to an obscuring of gender roles and inevitable conflict as each spouse focuses solely on his or her own needs rather than the needs of the marriage. "The confusion over roles is there, as are the legacies of a self-absorbed, me-first, feminist-do-or-die, male-backlash society," wrote Judith Wallerstein and Sandra Blakeslee in *The Good Marriage: How and Why Love Lasts.*[5]

Men's reaction to this phenomenon is twofold. They either give in to the new regime feminists have created, or they give up. Those who give in generally do so because they've either bought into the lie that women are just like men or because it's easier to get along with the women in their lives than to fight them.

The men who give up tend to remain silent, for if they speak out against feminism, they'll be labeled chauvinists. Many men would like to get married, but they know modern marriages are precarious. There's also no incentive for them to do so since they can have sex whenever they want and even live with their girlfriends with little interference from society. This was the theme of the movie *He's Just Not That Into You*. Two of the main characters, Neil and Beth, have been living together for seven years, but she dumps him when she realizes he isn't going to marry her. Rather than accept her share of the blame (by choosing to cohabitate in the first place), Beth suggests Neil is the bad guy for not wanting to get married.

He's Just Not That Into You is a splendid example of how feminism failed women. The sexual revolution was billed as something that would put women on par with men, but instead it has ruptured the male/female relationship. At first, women hesitate to get married because they think they'll lose their identities if they do; then when they *are* ready to get married (because their biological clocks are ticking), the men in their lives don't want to marry them.

That is hardly progress on the road to happiness.

The problem with the sexual revolution is that it was predicated on the lies that gender differences don't exist and that women want what men want. In fact, there was no need for a movement to make men and women equal because *they already were equal*—different, but equal. The reason female Democrats tell American women "there is still much work to be done," as Beth Frerking does in *Secrets of Powerful Women*, is that they refuse to admit feminism failed.[6] When you desperately want something to happen and it doesn't, there is always more work to be done. Women on the left are trying to force a square peg into a round hole.

Despite the failures of the feminist movement, it did have one powerful effect: it eradicated the power women once had over men! Before the 1960s, Americans understood that women had something men wanted, needed, and couldn't have without a woman's consent: sex and his own children. By equating sex with love, as women naturally do, men become better human beings—and society is better for it. "Without a durable relationship with a woman, a man's sexual life is a series of brief and temporary exchanges. With love, sex becomes refined by selectivity. The man himself is refined, and his sexuality becomes not a mere impulse but a commitment in society," wrote George Gilder in *Men and Marriage.*[7]

Now that feminism has eliminated men's need and desire to marry, the relationship between the sexes is unstable. Today, there are fewer reasons than ever for men to settle down—many are content to live for years with their girlfriends. Marriage often doesn't become an issue until one of the partners wants to have a baby. Some children come along before the decision whether or not to marry has been made!

Take Ben, for example. At forty, he lives with Julia, the mother of their child. She would like to get married (as most women do), but Ben claims he's content with the way things are. He loves Julia and their son, but he harbors a great deal of resentment toward this new world feminists have created. He knows most divorces are initiated by women and that men often have little say in the court system. Thus, he's concerned about what might happen should he and Julia ever get divorced.

Ben is also bitter about his single days and what he experienced in medical sales training. Throughout his twenties and most of his thirties, Ben struggled to find women with whom he could imagine settling down. None was interested in, or focused on, traditional marriage and motherhood. He got a doubly whammy when he entered the medical industry. "You should hear what they teach females while they're in school. They are indoctrinated to speak differently to males. They are always looking for ways to point out men's mistakes. Forget teamwork and performing to the best of one's ability within their scope of practice—just make life difficult for men."

Ben's biggest concern, however, is that Julia was raised by baby boomers with "far-left views." Though Julia herself is conservative, Ben is worried that her parents' influence, along with our liberal culture, will push Julia in that same direction.

Ben and Julia represent an extreme example of how feminism has affected the male/female bond. Most men aren't as strident in their beliefs as Ben, but many suffer in silence with the consequences of the feminist movement. By making men financially and biologically unnecessary, and by being dismissive of their needs and goals, men feel depleted—and some, like Ben, reject marriage altogether.

That isn't the answer, of course—particularly if men have, or want to have, children. Indeed, one of the best ways to counteract feminism is not to succumb to the world feminists have created but to specifically deny it. The only way to beat feminism is for women to reject the movement altogether and for men to marry women who do. Conservative women understand human nature, and they like men the way they are. They do not believe American women are oppressed, and they embrace marriage and motherhood and all that it entails—*including* taking their husbands' names. This attitude is a prerequisite for marriage.

Admittedly, beating feminists at their game is hard to do when everywhere we turn we're bombarded with feminist rhetoric. "I'd always had this feeling that if you got married, it was like the end of who you were," Sandra Bullock told Barbara Walters in a March 2010 interview.[8] Ms. Bullock is not an anomaly—such comments are standard fare in the media, and they represent how modern women have been taught to view marriage.

Ms. Bullock is a good example of the modern woman's conundrum. She made headlines about her split with Jesse

James. Though she is now known as the jilted wife of a philandering husband—and hailed in the media as the ultimate victim—the truth is more complex.

In post-feminist America, we readily accept and encourage women's power outside the home. But when the modern woman's personal life goes awry, all of a sudden she becomes a victim. Jesse James is guilty for his actions, of course, but why do we assume Ms. Bullock was a good wife? It's entirely possible—indeed, likely—that Ms. Bullock created a self-fulfilling prophecy. Having a negative attitude toward marriage beforehand, she no doubt got what she was expecting. Entering into marriage believing it'll be "the end of who you are" prevents a woman from making a good choice of partner and the emotional investment necessary to produce a successful marriage.

The message of media stories like Bullock's is clear: women are the folks who've been oppressed, victimized, and passed over for generations. They're the gender that's been held down, held back, and submissive for too long. So if a woman wants to be a famous actress and live in a state different from her husband for months at a time (or if she wants to be partner in a law firm or a senator or anything else that keeps her away from home for an extended period of time), well, then, her husband will just have to put up with it. And when he can't deal with it, as Jesse James obviously couldn't, he must be the bad guy—and she the victim. Even Laura Linney questions whether a guy can handle an actress's lifestyle which can mean going away for months at a time. She tells *More* Magazine, "Why should they?"

We don't know the details behind Jesse James and Sandra Bullock's marriage, of course, but the specifics aren't important to our analysis. What *is* important is the theme of today's marriages. Young people say they consider marriage a priority; but many don't have a solid grasp on why marriage is necessary, nor do they appreciate the many factors that can help make it a success. In an article titled "Tipper and Al Gore Separate: Congratulations to Them," the recently divorced *Girlfriends' Guide* author, Vicki Iovine, wrote, "Call me crazy, but I can't think of any other reason for people to marry than to raise kids or protect the monarchy."[9]

This attitude toward marriage—that it's unnecessary, or even undesirable—has become pervasive in the twenty-first century. A great deal of attention has been paid to the purpose of marriage after many public divorces recently made headlines: Jon and Kate Gosselin (of *Jon and Kate Plus Eight* fame); Tiger and Elin Woods; John and Elizabeth Edwards; the Bullocks; LeAnn Rimes; Larry King; and Al and Tipper Gore. Several weeks later, the Gores' daughter, Karenna Gore Schiff, announced her separation. All these trips to the courthouse don't help Americans in their quest to make marriage work. A study by James H. Fowler—author, social science researcher, and professor of political science at the University of California—found that if a sibling divorces, we are 22 percent more likely to divorce ourselves. And when our friends get divorced, it's even more influential: people who had a divorced friend were *147 percent more likely* to get divorced than people whose friends' marriages were intact! Apparently, peer pressure doesn't end in high school.

Living in a culture where divorce is approved by society makes it hard to stay married, but it's even harder when divorce is glorified. In the past several years, scores of articles have bemoaned marriage and exalted the benefits of divorce. In "Confessions of a Semi-Happy Wife," Ellen Tien has written, "Beneath the thumpingly ordinary nature of our marriage—Everymarriage—runs the silent chyron of divorce. It's the scarlet concept, the closely held contemplation of nearly every woman I know who has children who have been out of diapers for at least two years and a husband who won't be in them for another thirty."[10] Tien went on to extol the feminist message that women in previous generations "settled" by remaining in unhappy marriages. Thank God for divorce, wrote Tien, which "may be the last-standing woman's right to choose. . . . One eloquent swing of the ax and happiness is thrust firmly back into our own hands."[11]

But of all the writers who have ruminated over the state of modern marriage, Elizabeth Gilbert has been the most significant. Ms. Gilbert is the author of the memoir *Eat, Pray, Love,* which remained on the *New York Times* Best Seller list for 155 weeks and was made into a movie in 2010, starring Julia Roberts.

Gilbert's book tells the story of a thirty-something woman (Ms. Gilbert, ten years ago) looking for spirituality and happiness. She is married, but desperately unhappy. When she realizes the source of her discontent is that she doesn't want children (or, for that matter, to be married at all), she leaves her husband and falls into another relationship. When this relationship breaks up—as most rebound relationships are destined to do, particularly if you move in with your new lover, as Gilbert did—she is devastated. With a hefty advance from a publisher, Gilbert spends a year abroad—in Italy, India, and Indonesia—in an attempt to "find herself." But her story ends like any good romance novel: she finds Felipe instead.

Gilbert is a gifted writer. The prose in *Eat, Pray, Love* is exquisite, and the book has all the elements of a great story—except it isn't fiction. It is the story of Ms. Gilbert's life. But most women do not *genuinely* want to live her life. Her book simply provides an escape—and escapism sells. In real life, Gilbert's choices and desires are in stark contrast to the choices and desires of most women. Moreover, her attitude toward marriage is hopelessly doomed: she believes it threatens women's independence, as well as their well-being. Simply put, Ms. Gilbert is a feminist. She could be Virginia Woolf's best friend.

When we talk about America's culture war, what we're often really talking about is women and their role in society. Bill O'Reilly, television's foremost culture warrior, fails to drive home this point on *The O'Reilly Factor*. He prides himself on covering topics the other networks won't, but even he treads carefully when it comes to women and feminism. Often, his strategy is to deflect the situation or simply be caustic. The constant avoidance by those in the media means the only people Americans hear from when it comes to women's issues are feminists. Yet they are the last people in the world from whom American women—who are primarily a conservative bunch—should be taking advice.

When asked in an interview what she makes of the remarkable success of *Eat, Pray, Love*, Gilbert admits to being flummoxed. She says she can't understand why Oprah Winfrey would devote two entire programs to her book, or why the book prompted women to tell her she inspired them to get divorced. Her editor, Paul Slovak, thinks he knows: "Somehow the book was really well timed in terms of an entire generation of women who perhaps didn't want to live in accord with the expectations of American society."[12] *Washington Post* staff writer Ellen McCarthy adds, "*Eat, Pray, Love* became [women's] handbook, and Gilbert their guide."[13]

This analysis is wrongheaded. The modern generation is not looking to circumvent the expectations of marriage and motherhood—*Gilbert* is. Women loved her book, but that does not equate to identification; the book is simply a great read because it's a good story, and it's well written.

The success of *Eat, Pray, Love* is an excellent example of the insidiousness of the feminist culture. The media elite love stories like Ms. Gilbert's because of the statement it makes about men, marriage, and female identity. Any story that portrays women as victims, or portrays women in search of their identity in the absence of husband and children, is a shoo-in for mainstream media publicity. That's why Oprah basked in Ms. Gilbert's glory. Oprah doesn't believe in traditional marriage either—nor does she want children: "Marriage means to me offering—sacrificing—yourself to the relationship. I'm not capable of doing that."[14] Sounds awfully similar to the statement Gilbert made in an interview for *O* magazine: "I saw [marriage] as oppressive and outdated. And stupid and useless. And possibly very, very destructive."[15]

What women in the media do is a scam. Myrna Blyth, former editor of *Ladies' Home Journal*, exposes this fact in her book, *Spin Sisters*. "Spin sisters are members of the female media elite, a Girls' Club of editors, producers, and print and television journalists with similar attitudes and opinions who influence the way millions of American women think and feel about their lives, their world, and themselves."[16] And they do it under the false notion that they are just like everyone else.

Sugar Rautbord, a fellow Chicagoan who knew Oprah long before she became a millionaire media mogul, told Kitty Kelley, "[Oprah] figured out early that the only way to have a successful career and make money—big money—was to delete husbands and children and carpools from life's agenda. None of these problems touch Oprah in the golden sphere in which she lives. Yet she still addresses our issues of husbands and children and carpools as if they were her issues, as if she really is Everywoman."[17]

Ms. Gilbert is just as dishonest. Her best-selling sequel, *Committed: A Skeptic Makes Peace with Marriage*, suggests that the reservations she once had about marriage have been quelled—but they have not. She and her lover Felipe from the end of *Eat, Pray, Love*, do not fall in love and decide to marry, as the book implies. Rather, they are "sentenced to wed" due to Felipe's status as an illegal alien. If the couple wanted to continue living in the United States, or ever visit the United States, they *had* to get married—and Ms. Gilbert was resentful, for she had sworn off marriage altogether.

Knowing this would not make for a good book, she (or her editors) lured the readers of *Eat, Pray, Love* to *Committed* by implying it would have a happy ending. In fact, the book is a left-wing diatribe. Gilbert questions the purpose of marriage at every turn and blames conservatives for keeping women down. She carefully avoids the term *liberal*—thus making her case for feminism even more insidious—but repeatedly uses the term *conservative* as though it were a bad word.

Gilbert's background, which she details in *Committed*, sheds light on why she is such a confused young woman. In one passage, she wrote, "I was raised to believe I was special. . . . My 'me-ness' was always prized. . . . With the possible exception of the very most conservative families among us, everyone I knew—at some basic level—shared this assumed cultural respect for the individual. . . . The pursuit of happiness was my natural . . . birthright."[18]

Ironically, Gilbert's assessment of her upbringing identifies what's wrong with the modern generation. It's precisely *because* conservative families don't raise their children the way Gilbert was raised that they don't end up with narcissistic children who have little regard for the institution of marriage. Gilbert's point—that conservative families don't value individualism— is ridiculous. Parents can respect their children's individuality and at the same time impart traditional values.

Committed demonstrates what has happened over the past few decades as a new generation of women came of age. This is the generation that was raised to be self-centered and autonomous. When (and if) baby boomer parents gave their children advice, they did so tentatively, as though the advice were simply opinion rather than something they learned the hard way to be a bona fide fact. As we learned in the last chapter, baby boomers left their children alone to figure things out for themselves. The result is a generation of women who have no idea how to make healthy decisions when it comes to love, sex, and marriage. Or, as in Gilbert's case, they ruminate for years over decisions they do make.

Another interesting statement Gilbert made—in *Eat, Pray, Love*—is this: "It was my most sincere belief when I left my husband that we could settle our practical affairs in a few hours with a calculator, some common sense, and a bit of goodwill toward the person we'd once loved."[19] Somewhere along the line, either from her parents or the culture, Gilbert got the impression that getting divorced is no big deal. This is yet another example of the modern generation's immaturity and defeatist attitude toward marriage.

In fairness to modern women, it *is* harder to be married today than it used to be. Being happily married requires a climate that's conducive to this goal—and we don't have it. But just because something is harder than it should be doesn't mean it's hopeless. Writing books that slam the institution of marriage, glorify divorce, and encourage women to do what Ms. Gilbert did is hardly beneficial. It merely leads to more unhappiness and discontent.

Marriage is indeed undergoing much scrutiny in America, but its purpose and benefits, as well as people's desire for it, remain intact. *Do not listen to the women in the media.* The institution of marriage isn't the problem—we are. Simply put, we've messed up. "There is no other single force causing as much measurable hardship and human misery in this country as the collapse of marriage," wrote Caitlin Flanagan in *Time.*[20]

How, then, do we move forward—not necessarily to achieve a perfect marriage, but at least to increase our chance of marital success? By choosing the right spouse, aligning our expectations with reality, becoming well versed in gender differences, and changing our attitude. Let's begin with the latter.

CHANGING OUR ATTITUDE

The single greatest obstacle young people face when it comes to marriage is their attitude. Since the day they were born, they have been taught two basic tenets about marriage: that it doesn't have to be permanent, and that it is not an institution to which young people, women in particular, should aspire. Instead, they should focus on getting to know themselves as individuals—figure out who they are, what they want out of life, and what they need in a spouse. Then, and only then, should they get married.

But what does it mean to know oneself in a culture in which people take twice as long as they should to grow up? Maturity is a prerequisite for marriage, yes. But there is no evidence that today's young people spend their single years in pursuit of this goal. Most spend their days working and their nights watching television. According to the *Wall Street Journal*, television "ranks after sleep and work as the activity Americans devote the most time to."[21] Many also drink excessively during these years, and either hook up or live with their partners in a perpetual state of uncertainty—neither of which prepares them for a life of matrimony.

Indeed, the irony of the "finding oneself" argument is that it is marriage—not the single life—that allows people to discover who they are. By being accountable to another person, a spouse learns what he or she is capable of. Only by making sacrifices can we grow as individuals.

That doesn't mean everyone should get married in their twenties—how ready people are for marriage depends on how they were raised. Were they taught to be responsible, mature adults? Were they taught that sacrifice in life is inevitable, even good? Or were they encouraged to listen to their inner voices, do what's best for themselves, focus on their careers, and have lots of different sexual experiences? Indeed, Americans have confused the concept of getting to know oneself with the real problem: poor role models. Not only has the modern generation been raised in a divorce culture, but their parents taught them values that don't bode well for marriage.

In the past, Americans viewed marriage as the beginning of their lives, not the end. Getting married and having a family was a good thing, a positive thing, something people got excited about—and the culture supported this goal. Then the sexual revolution came along and changed everything. Feminists argued that men got the better end of the marriage deal, and that marriage oppresses women and keeps them from realizing their true potential. They accomplished their goal by assuring women their biology is no different from a man's. They agreed that men and women have different sex organs, but they claimed there's nothing else that separates the sexes. It's the culture, feminists said, that makes women think they want to get married and have babies. If American women weren't oppressed, they would see that what they want out of life is exactly what men want.

Feminists have no understanding of what makes men and women tick—turning to them for advice is like seeking advice from a pediatrician because your car won't start. American women have been receiving guidance *from the wrong people.* Even those who say they aren't feminists believe women should be as powerful as men outside the home—that's what was taught to them by their parents, by their schools and colleges, and by the media. The idea of freeing women from the supposed cultural stereotypes prevails even as feminism itself appears irrelevant.

The other way in which the modern generation's attitude is harmful is that they enter into marriage thinking they can always get divorced. This is a mistake. Any good psychologist will admit that one's approach often determines the outcome. "The very option of being allowed to change our minds seems to increase the chances we *will* change our minds. When we can change our minds about decisions, we are less satisfied with them. When a decision is final, we engage in a variety of psychological processes that enhance our feelings about the choice we made relative to the alternatives," wrote Barry Schwartz in *The Paradox of Choice*.[22]

One of the most important things women can do to improve their chances of marital success is become educated about the differences between men and women. Fortunately, there has been an extraordinary amount of data gathered regarding gender differences in the last several years. There has never been a better time for women and men to truly understand one another.

UNDERSTANDING THE DIFFERENCE

Since marriage involves the union of a man and a woman who will presumably share the same space for decades, it stands to reason that a thorough understanding of the sexes should be in place. Before feminists started waging a war against human nature, Americans had a keen awareness of the opposite sex. They didn't know *why* men and women were different, but they knew they were. They understood what the modern generation does not: men have their role and women have theirs—and each is equally powerful and important. In fact, it is *women* who have the upper hand when it comes to gender relations.

How so? "The crucial process of civilization is the subordination of male sexual impulses and biology to the long-term horizons of female sexuality," wrote George Gilder. "In creating civilization, women transform male lust into love; channel wanderlust into jobs, homes, and families; link men to specific children; rear children into citizens; and change hunters to fathers. The prime fact of life is the sexual superiority of women."[23]

These words are foreign to young people. They have never heard anyone suggest women are the superior sex. On the contrary, they've been told women are inferior. That's why the word *power*, or *empowerment*, is so important to them. Rarely does a week go by that we do not hear power associated with women. We certainly don't hear it associated with men! To suggest men want power, or should even have power, is verboten. Power is women's domain. They deserve it because they (supposedly) never had it.

But they did. Women of yesteryear had enormous power, just of a different variety. Today when we talk about power, we're referring to money and status. That makes sense, for this kind of power reflects modern values. In the past, when marriage and family took center stage, women were exalted on the home front. Husbands deferred to wives on virtually all household matters, including child rearing. Women were revered for their unique sensibilities.

When women usurp men's role in society, as they do now, it messes up the order of things. Most men don't want to compete with women; they want to take care of them. It makes men feel important and boosts their self-esteem. What's more, statistics prove women want men to have the dominant role in the relationship. Recognizing this doesn't give men carte blanche to treat women as subordinate—and most men don't do this, or want to do this. That's a feminist scare tactic to convince women otherwise.

Today, if a person even *alludes* to the traditional male/female dance—especially if it's a man—there is hell to pay. In 2006, *Forbes* editor Michael Noer wrote an article titled "Don't Marry Career Women," which sent feminists into a tizzy and prompted a rebuttal from Noer's coworker, Elizabeth Corcoran. The point of Noer's article was to highlight the social science research that proves career women, defined as those who work more than thirty-five hours a week, are "more likely to divorce, less likely to have children, and if they do have kids, are more likely to be unhappy about it."[24] Noer concedes that many employed mothers are happily married; he simply points out that studies show they're *less likely to be so* than mothers who are not employed.

He also highlights a study that found *both* men and women are unhappy when wives make more money than their husbands. This is an inconvenient truth, to be sure; but that doesn't make it any less true. It seems that despite women's desire for independence, they still want to be taken care of—and money is part of that equation.

When women insist on competing with men at the same level, which is what happens when a society adopts the feminist view that men and women are the same, conflict ensues. It rears its ugly head as a logistical issue—as couples face the stress of both spouses having heavy workloads—and it rears its ugly head in the bedroom. It seems that highly educated couples who both spend their days at the office are more likely to cheat. "When your spouse works outside the home, chances increase that he or she will meet someone more likable than you," wrote Noer.[25] This is not to suggest women shouldn't be in the marketplace. But it *is* to say ramifications ensue when husbands and wives are both subjected to temptations on a consistent basis.

The marriages that stand the best chance of survival (and appear happiest) are those in which husbands and wives are not competing. Traditional marriages, in which wives depend on their husbands' incomes and husbands defer to their wives on matters related to the home—including how to spend his income—are generally in harmony. Even in households in which women *do* work outside the home, smart wives don't bring their professional selves home. They may wield some measure of power in the marketplace; but when they get home, these women take on a more traditional role.

The reversal of gender roles in modern America has been disastrous. It's great that men spend more time with their kids than their own fathers did, and it's great that modern advances have allowed women to be successful outside the home. But neither of these developments should eradicate the delicate balance between husbands and wives. They can each take part in the other's primary role without supplanting it. That should be the goal.

Of all the ways to improve the relationship between the sexes, none is more important than accepting—and embracing—gender differences. Until we understand who men and women are as individuals and how they work in tandem, we will never be happy.

ALIGNING EXPECTATIONS WITH REALITY

Since modern women have been raised to believe they're the center of the universe and deserve a gilded life, it isn't surprising they have inflated expectations of marriage. Lori Gottlieb, author of *Marry Him: The Case for Settling for Mr. Good Enough*, urges women to take a good look at their dating habits. She suggests the problem is not a dearth of good men but women's expectations for finding the perfect man. A single woman in her forties, Gottlieb learned the hard way that modern women—herself included—expect too much. Many walk away from perfectly good relationships based on a *feeling* that they can find someone better.

But not only are feelings unreliable; women's choices dwindle as they get older—and before they realize it, it's too late. As one Amazon reviewer of Ms. Gottlieb's book wrote, "I was raised by a mother who told me I was beautiful and only deserved the most textbook Mr. Right. So for most of my dating life, I've discarded dozens of guys for not immediately making me go all starry-eyed."[26]

Ms. Gottleib's book hit a nerve. Coincidentally, it was published on the heels of a study by the National Bureau of Economic Research, titled "The Paradox of Declining Female Happiness." Authors Betsey Stevenson and Justin Wolfers suggest the feminist movement raised women's expectations faster than society was able to meet them. "As women's expectations move into alignment with their experiences, this decline in happiness may reverse."[27]

Women also have ridiculously high expectations of sex. They've been exposed to an array of sexual images their entire lives and imagine sex to be something different from what it is. Sex is not the be-all-end-all. It is one part of life—and not necessarily a huge part. It depends on the two people in the marriage and what stage of life they're in: Do they have children or not? How old are the children? Are both spouses employed, or is one of the spouses at home, helping to produce a less stressful environment? Numerous factors go into how often people have sex and what kind of sex they have. Unfortunately, the younger generation has been raised to believe that any good relationship must enjoy movielike sex at all times. But as Raquel Welch wrote in her autobiography, *Raquel: Beyond the Cleavage*, "Sex is overrated and constantly hyped far beyond what it can deliver. If you're lucky, it occurs with some regularity—but it's not the whole enchilada."[28]

Had women not been raised under the banner of "girl power" and empowerment, they wouldn't have landed in such a precarious position. Women should accept that in fact they are *not* special. In the groundbreaking book *Nurtureshock*—hailed by the media as "revolutionary"—authors Po Bronson and Ashley Merryman describe what they call the "inverse power of praise." Their book demonstrates that overpraising one's kids in an attempt to boost their self-esteem is, in fact, harmful. "Sure, [your child] is special. But new research suggests that if you tell him that, you'll ruin him. It's a neurobiological fact."[29]

Indeed, America's incessant focus on women's issues—which suggest women are so distinguished that they require special attention—has produced a generation of inflated egos. The truth is that women are simply *one piece* of a very large pie— they make up part of a family. Men and children are just as valuable, and they have their own set of needs and expectations.

How to Choose a Spouse

Historically, for a woman the notion of "choosing well" is associated with marrying a man with a promising career. For a man it means choosing a woman he'd want to bring home to meet Mom. Since human nature doesn't change, these factors are still important to men and women, but few admit it.

We're not supposed to. Since it is assumed women are no different from men, women are no longer taught to look for a stable, career-oriented guy. The plan is for women to support *themselves*. The only women who think to look for a guy who makes a decent income, or who has the ability and drive to make a good income, are the women who know they plan to stay home with their children.

But most women today do not plan to do this. They have

been groomed for another life altogether. Whether or not they eventually quit their jobs to stay home when they discover how demanding babies are, they don't *assume* beforehand that they will do this. The result is that women often ignore a boyfriend's financial potential.

In the past, mothers warned their daughters to look for men who can provide for them. They correctly assumed their daughter would be out of the workforce for some period of time and thus would need a husband who could provide for her and their future children. That's what happened to Lori Gottlieb, the single mother author who warns women not to do what she did. When Gottlieb was dating boyfriends whose financial prospects were bleak, her (smart) mother asked her if these men would be able to support a family. "At the time, I thought she was such a throwback to the '50s, so old-fashioned and unenlightened and out of touch with women of my generation. But it turns out she was right."[30]

Indeed, love does not pay the bills—nor does it allow women to stay home with their babies. But the average woman hasn't been taught to think in these terms. She worries only about herself and considers dependence on a man to be a bad thing. After she matures and has children, however, she begins to feel resentful. This is understandable, since she has, in effect, been lied to her entire life by just about every woman she knows. With all the talk of women's independence, no one ever suggested she might *want* to stay home!

Women also ignore red flags. Sandra Bullock dismissed the fact that her philandering ex-husband had previously been married to a porn star! Women in previous generations had a better grasp on how to weed out the bad guys—in part because their parents weren't afraid to give their children advice. Some parents even played matchmaker in an attempt to help their adult children make good choices—older adults can often anticipate the kinds of things young people will face down the road. Matchmaking may seem preposterous today, but there were practical reasons for it.

Geography is another aspect of the modern relationship that causes couples anguish. In our transient society, women move far away from their hometowns to go to college, which increases the likelihood that they'll fall in love with someone from another state. If women settle far from their families of origin, their own mothers will not be available to help women care for their children when they have them. This isn't something couples think about when they're making plans to marry; but after a few years, it becomes critical.

Finally, it is imperative that couples determine how they plan to raise a family. Regardless of how carefully women plan their lives, the truth is that children will rock their world. In many cases, whatever plans women had go out the window once they're holding their own babies. That's why couples should discuss ahead of time their values and expectations about family life. While plans are subject to change, knowing each person's ideal is key—many married couples find themselves stuck with lives they hadn't prepared for because they never discussed the matter beforehand. Since dual-income families have become the new norm, couples assume that with a little ingenuity, this lifestyle is perfectly manageable. Not until they become parents do they realize they were wrong.

· 5 ·

WHEN MOTHERS WORK

If you chase two rabbits, you will not catch either one.

—Russian proverb

Emotionally, this is a difficult chapter to read—so first, two caveats. Our position on what the media call "working mothers"—an absurd and misleading term since mothers at home work harder than anyone—is *not* that all children whose mothers are employed are doomed. Nor do we suggest that all children whose mothers stay home flourish. Clearly, there are a host of factors that contribute to a child's well-being. That this is true, however, does not change the fact that the mass exodus of mothers from the home over the past thirty years—which was, and continues to be, a main feminist objective—has been devastating.

Second, the greatest problem we face as a nation when it comes to this issue is that the media refuse to address the gigantic chasm among various *kinds* of "working," or employed, mothers. Are we talking about mothers whose children are all in school, or mothers of babies and toddlers? Are we talking about mothers who work full-time, year-round (and may also have an hour or two of commuting) or mothers who work part-time, which can mean as few as ten hours per week, or mothers who have home-based employment? Are we talking about children who spend long hours in day care or children who attend day care only several hours a day? Are we talking about grandmothers, or other trusted individuals, who provide *consistent* care to one or several children?

These distinctions are critical—we cannot discuss the topic of "working mothers" without distinguishing among these various scenarios. Why? Because we now know from research that *the most important aspect* of a child's early life is that he has the consistent care and attention of one individual—preferably the mother, but not necessarily. Naturally, this is not something that can occur in a large group setting. (It could occur, however, in small, in-home care by a trusted friend or relative.) "Good daycare vs. bad daycare is not the issue. Full-time daycare, good or bad, can and usually does interfere with the fundamental emotional development of young children," wrote authors and former day care owners William and Wendy Dreskin.[1]

We acknowledge the chasm that exists among these various circumstances. Therefore, this chapter focuses exclusively on mothers who have remained in the workforce consistently throughout their lives and placed their children in full-time group care.

According to the nonpartisan polling agency, Public Agenda, 70 percent of parents with children under age five agree that "having a parent at home is best." In addition, 63 percent disagree with the idea that children in day care receive "just as good" care and attention as with a stay-at-home parent. Even more alarming is this fact: six in ten Americans rate their generation "fair" or "poor" in raising children.

Clearly, something has gone very wrong. And though there may be various culprits—the breakdown of the family, for example—it is indisputable that the feminist push to get mothers, particularly mothers of young children, out of the home and into the workforce full-time has been a disastrous social experiment.

You've probably never heard it put in these terms. That's because the women in the media are hopelessly biased when it comes to this issue. It is *the most personal topic* they could potentially cover—which is why they don't. Bernard Goldberg was the first to explain why in his groundbreaking book, *Bias*—the premier exposé of the biases of the media elite. In it, Goldberg devotes an entire chapter to "the most important story you never saw on TV," which refers to the female media executives who are fiercely hostile to any criticism of employed mothers or day care. These women have made it taboo for the media to report or debate the social costs of this phenomenon.

"It's not that there's been a television news blackout on all the bad things happening to our kids; it's that the elite journalists have no desire to connect the dots. They don't report the really big story—arguably one of the biggest stories of our time—that this absence of mothers from the home is without any historical precedent, and that millions upon millions of American children have been left, as Mary Eberstadt puts it [in her book *Home-Alone America*] to 'fend for themselves'—with dire consequences," wrote Goldberg.[2]

Why do the feminist elite ignore this subject? For two reasons. First, most of the women in the media are working mothers themselves—they drop their children off at day care or leave them with a nanny every morning before they report to their job. Thus, they are hardly in a position to address the topic in an unbiased manner. Doing so would make them feel like bad mothers and would require a major overhaul in the way they've been taught to think about women and work— and they're not about to do this. Simply put, the feminist elite are incapable of making the parallel between children's well-being and the absence of mothers from the home.

CONNECTING THE DOTS

Nevertheless, here is what we know: For the first time in American history, parents are no longer expected to care for the children they bring into this world. In the past, it was expected that parents would raise their own children—farming this task out to hired help was something only wealthy families did. The reason was not that women "in those days" were oppressed, or because families could "afford" to do so, as feminists would have you believe. It was because Americans appreciated the fact that children have needs, and that these needs are best met by their own parents.

Then feminists came along and undermined the value of motherhood. They spread the message that motherhood isn't a suitable career goal for educated women. Women, they said, should make careers—not children—the focus of their lives. Substitute caregivers, in other words, are perfectly capable of doing what mothers have historically done for free.

And women listened.

Thirty years later, here's what we have to show for it: an enormous rise in emotional problems among even the very young; an epidemic of defiant schoolchildren, to the point where anti-bullying programs have become commonplace; a triple increase in childhood obesity; chronic sleep deprivation; a marked increase in premarital and sexual activity; an almost total lack of exposure to nature and healthy exercise; and, most important, a complete collapse of parental discipline.

We should note that today's parenting experience differs sharply from thirty years ago. Indeed, the vast majority of parents in America—76 percent—believe raising children today is "a lot harder" than when they were growing up. Today's moms and dads are fighting a culture that directly restricts the parenting process. Between desolate neighborhoods and the myriad of technological devices and media messages thrust on children, it's amazing parents survive the experience intact. Nevertheless, we have a choice. Do we continue to go down the road we're on, or do we begin to reverse the process?

We are *not* suggesting we can go back to the way things were, as leftists will be quick to point out. But we *are* suggesting we look back at where we went wrong—because here's a sobering fact: society may change, but children don't. They come into this world today with the same needs and expectations as they did one hundred years ago, and parents continue to be *the most significant influence* in their lives.

For this reason alone, we must find the answer.

In *The Myth of Multitasking*, management expert Dave Crenshaw addresses the popular concept known as multitasking. Using a modern-day fable, Crenshaw becomes "Phil," a coaching consultant. Phil is assigned to teach Helen, an executive who prides herself on her multitasking skills, why multitasking is a lie. He begins with its definition: *the apparent simultaneous performance of two or more tasks by a computer's central processing unit.* "Multitasking was first a computer term," he tells Helen. "The word *apparent* in that definition is very important. Just like your brain, the computer can't focus on two or more things at the same time. What the processor is really doing is switching rapidly between one program and the other—giving the illusion that it's doing it all at the same time."[3]

Helen isn't convinced. She has been multitasking her entire life and depends on it to accomplish everything she has to do.

Each time Phil provides examples from Helen's life to demonstrate why her approach isn't effective, Helen becomes defensive. By the end of the book, however, Phil manages to convince Helen that she's merely switchtasking—turning away from one thing to focus on another—rather than multitasking, which suggests she's accomplishing more than one thing at a time. It takes the entire book to convince her; but in the final chapter, Helen is ready and willing to give up the entire notion of multitasking.

The message of Crenshaw's book is that the human brain is like a computer: it is only capable of focusing on one thing at a time. Switching back and forth between different tasks cannot overcome the brain's inability to process two sets of information simultaneously. Multitasking wastes time and money, and damages our relationships at work and at home. Thus, it is a myth.

But don't expect the modern generation to embrace this fact—today's women have been groomed for a life of multitasking. Since childhood, they've been told they can have everything they want in life all at the same time. Their mentors didn't use the word *multitasking*, but that's exactly what they suggested women do. Pursuing a full-time career alongside of motherhood, at least when children are young, is an attempt at multitasking.

The modern generation is the first to try this impossible task. In the past, women viewed their lives as sequential. In the 1944 movie *National Velvet*, the mother says to her daughter (played by Elizabeth Taylor), "There's a time for everything—all in proper order, and in proper time." This outlook allowed women to have it all, but not simultaneously—and that's a critical difference. Women also understood that they were different from men and, because of this, had a unique and important obligation at home. Being mothers didn't mean they couldn't pursue other interests or jobs, but women were not encumbered with the daunting task of trying to do every-thing at once.

Feminists want you to think the reason mothers in the past didn't do what mothers do today is because women were oppressed. But the real reason women planned their lives accordingly is because they were less focused on themselves and more concerned with the greater good, and part of the greater good meant taking responsibility for one's children. Modern women, on the other hand, have been taught to focus on their own needs—what *they* want is what matters most in life. So if women don't want to, or "choose" to, stay home with their children, they shouldn't have to.

Despite this change in attitude, the majority of Americans continue to believe one parent should stay home in children's early years and be available after school for their older children. But you wouldn't know this from turning on your television sets or reading women's magazines. To hear the media tell it, most mothers today "work" and have no choice in the matter. Even worse, we're told, mothers are expected to do a double shift. They must earn an income, plus do all the work involved in raising children and maintaining a household.

That these women are overwhelmed is obvious. Who wouldn't be? When mothers work full-time outside the home, they have no time to perform the myriad of tasks homemakers have traditionally done—such as care for babies and toddlers; plan, shop, and prepare three healthy meals a day; do the laundry; oversee homework; run errands; attend school func-tions; transport children to various activities; take children to their doctors' appointments; take care of aging parents; and organize the couple's social life. All these things fall by the way-side when both parents are employed full-time. Only those who can afford household help are largely free from such worries.

But most of the employed mothers we hear from blame

husbands for not pulling their weight. Yet husbands are doing precisely what their wives are doing! Fathers feel the time crunch just as mothers do. (What a concept!) The issue is not, as feminists claim, that husbands are clueless about what needs to be done at home (though this may be the case for some). The issue is that neither spouse has the time to perform these other tasks when they're both consumed by demanding careers. In other words, the system itself is ineffective—not the people in it.

The result of this new world feminists have created looks something like this:

From the *New York Times*: "I find [marriage and motherhood] to be pretty darn impossible. Or, at least, I find doing well at both of them to be impossible. Not to mention working, too."
—Cathy C.

From a *Newsweek* Web Exclusive: "Modern motherhood isn't hard; it's impossible. There are just simply not enough hours in the day to do everything. I'm serious. It's a rigged game."

From another *Newsweek* Web Exclusive: "When I was younger I felt misled by the pervasive theme that women can do it all. In observing myself and my friends and colleagues, it is much more difficult—if not impossible—in reality."— "southflmom"

Such comments are standard fare in the media. Indeed, how to balance work and family is the premier topic of women's magazines. Round and round the editors go—month after month, year after year—trying to come up with yet another new plan that will help women multitask effectively. But nothing ever works. Instead, women's attempt to balance full-time careers with motherhood has created conflict in the home and even crippled their ability to enjoy life.

In response to this, some have begun to reject the notion that women can "have it all." In 2003, author and *New York Times* columnist Lisa Belkin wrote an article called "The Opt-Out Revolution." It refers to the percentage of highly educated women who leave the workforce to stay home with their children.

"Arguably, the barriers of 40 years ago are down. Fifty percent of the undergraduate class of 2003 at Yale was female; this year's graduating class at Berkeley Law School was 63 percent women; Harvard was 46 percent; Columbia was 51. Nearly 47 percent of medical students are women, as are 50 percent of undergraduate business majors. They are recruited by top firms in all fields. They start strong out of the gate," wrote Belkin. "And then, suddenly, they stop." [4]

As Belkin explains, women make up only 16 percent of partners in law firms and 16 percent of corporate officers. Moreover, only eight companies in the Fortune 500 have female CEOs, and of 435 members of the House of Representatives and the 100-member Senate, only 62 and 14, respectively, are women. Belkin uses these figures to represent "a revolution stalled."

Why did it stall? For the same reason we talked about in Chapter 2: women are realizing they're not willing to put in the hours required to make it to the top.

It is, of course, important to note that some women do forge ahead, and, in spite of it all, are successful. (It is also worth noting that the more successful women are, the fewer children they tend to have.) But the women who do not opt out of the workforce *despite being overwhelmed* tend to be women whose choices are governed by feminist ideology, and the primary source of their angst is guilt.

WORKING MOM GUILT

The magazine *Working Mother* prides itself on helping women balance work and family, but reading its articles is an exercise in futility. Moreover, no delineation is made between balancing school-age children with part-time (or even full-time) work and balancing babies and toddlers with full-time work. To the editors at *Working Mother*, both scenarios constitute one category. This demonstrates a profound lack of understanding as to what's involved in caring for children since the early years are clearly more physically draining and time-consuming than the later years. It isn't surprising the feminist elite don't make this distinction, since most have never been home with their children long enough to appreciate it.

That's why the editors are tormented by guilt. Almost every issue examines a new aspect of this modern phenomenon. For example, the May 2010 issue of *Working Mother* featured an article on the cover titled, "Will My Child Turn Out Okay?" In the following issue, the cover story was titled "Never feel GUILTY again!" This magazine is so consumed with guilt it might as well be called *Guilt-Free Living*.

In one of the articles, Inara Verzemnieks wrote about a working mother who remembers the day her "heart broke." Apparently the day care provider told her she had "put her children's cots together at naptime so they could comfort each other through tears."[5] Another mother Verzemnieks interviewed said the nagging feeling she gets that she could have done things differently never goes away.

In another article, Ilisa Cohen describes a typical day in Michelle Dubanowski's life. Dubanowski works full-time, has a preschooler and a three-month-old, and amid the madness forgets to attend her son's "graduation" from preschool. This story segues into the theme of Cohen's article: "All working moms have guilt war stories."[6]

Cohen explains that she and the editors at *Working Mother* "went on an exploratory mission" to try to understand "the anatomy of guilt." They spoke with experts (one wonders which experts they consulted—guilt experts?) to determine why working mothers are fraught with guilt and what they can do to make it go away so they can sleep at night. They also want to know why men don't suffer from this malady.

This is nuts. Modern women are drowning and desperately searching for a lifeboat. By refusing to believe they cannot have it all simultaneously, they are inflicting themselves with mental anguish. They are also forcing themselves to ignore their children's cries and seek validation from the culture. Actress Alison Sweeney—who tapes *Days of Our Lives* three days a week and *The Biggest Loser* three to four days a week—told her pediatrician that her son pleads with her to stay with him. The pediatrician told her not to worry—children behave this way "even if you're a stay-at-home mom going to the grocery store."[7]

That is absolutely false. Most children whose mothers are home do not suffer from the kind of separation anxiety and sadness that children of full-time employed mothers do. Even America's pediatricians have buckled under the pressure from our feminist society, though few will admit it. Until women realize their guilt is their conscience talking to them, they will continue to sink further in the sea.

To be fair, this phenomenon isn't entirely their fault. The culture of moral relativity in which women have been raised didn't teach them to think in terms of right and wrong, so when they're confronted by their conscience—which is what guilt is—women try to push it away. They don't realize, or they refuse to accept, that their conscience is telling them what they're doing is a bad idea.

Guilt has been made far more complicated than it is. There are essentially two kinds of guilt mothers feel: real guilt, the kind that eats away at you because you know you've done something wrong and your conscience isn't letting you off the hook, and unfounded guilt, the kind that rears its ugly head at a mother's slightest misstep but is, for the most part, fleeting and irrational. It is certainly natural for mothers to want to do right by their children, which is why women sometimes worry that any mishap will cause their children irreparable harm. But it won't. There is plenty of room for human error when it comes to parenting, which seems to be something fathers know instinctively.

Angered by the fact that fathers don't suffer from the same type of insecurities mothers do, women try to be more like men. They think women should be able to have babies, leave them in other people's care, and not feel bad about it. Moreover, society supports—and even glorifies—this practice. Our culture assists women in assuaging their guilt by assuring them such feelings are spurious, the result of an oppressive society.

A striking example is an interview in *Cookie* magazine with authors Alicia Ybarco and Mary Ann Zoellner, producers of the *Today* show. In describing their lives, the two women explain that their job is very demanding. "The hours can be crazy. There've been times I've come home to feed the baby and put her to sleep, then gone back to work until 4 a.m.," said Zoellner, to which Ybarco added, "There isn't a day that goes by that I don't wonder, Could I have given more to the job? Could I have done more with my family? The guilt is there wherever you go—it's just a matter of whether you choose to listen to it."[8]

Think about that. Modern women are forcing themselves, with society's blessing, to ignore their conscience. That is no small matter.

There is no way to feel serious, debilitating guilt if there is nothing to feel guilty about. A woman who cannot rid herself of guilt, whose heart feels as though it is being crushed, has simply made a bad decision. That is the nature of guilt. The only reason the definition has become skewed is that women try to find a way to avoid their guilt, justify their guilt, or blame their guilt on society. "Guilt is good for absolutely nothing but perpetuating unhappiness. So forget the guilt—there's nothing to be guilty about," wrote Cathy L. Greenberg, PhD and Barrett Avigdor, JD.[9]

Such statements are par for the course in the media; and they're almost always made by women with impressive academic degrees, making the words more powerful. If a professional says it, or so the thinking goes, it must be true. Yet these so-called experts have no concept of children's needs. American women have been getting an earful about motherhood from those who know the least about it!

When powerful women, such as CNN's Campbell Brown, quit their jobs to stay home, the feminist elite assures us these women were forced out. They're victims, we're told, of America's outdated policies that fail to cater to women's needs. But Brown offered an explanation that implies she listened to the voice that was talking to her: "My plan right now is to help CNN through any transition—and then to enjoy, for the very first time, the nightly ritual of *Good Night Moon* and goodnight kisses with my two little boys. I wish my CNN colleagues all the best. As long as bedtime doesn't conflict with primetime, I will be watching and pulling for them."[10]

Katherine Heigl of the hit television series *Grey's Anatomy* was more forthright in her explanation for why she quit the series mid-season. Heigl explained that she could no longer "sacrifice [her] relationship with [her] child." She says she felt terrible about leaving the show and should have planned things better but does not want to "disappoint" her child. "I had to make a choice. You wish you could have it all exactly the way you want it, but that's not life."[11]

THE TWO-INCOME ARGUMENT: A RED HERRING

For some time, the prevailing wisdom in America has been that most mothers *have to* work, but what does "having to work" mean? Clearly, if a woman has children to support and she isn't married, she must provide an income. And, yes, the rate of single mothers has hit an all-time high of 40 percent, which means more unmarried mothers are in the workforce than ever before.

But to the degree that a *married* mother has to work depends on various factors. The spin sisters make it sound as though modern women are victims of the economy, as though most mothers want to be home but can't be. Yet nothing happened *to* married mothers to drive them into the workforce—the way the death or unemployment of a spouse might. *Feminists created an environment that demanded it.* "All the income growth in the U.S. since 1970 has come from women working outside the home," wrote Bridget Brennan in *Why She Buys.*[12]

Note the date: 1970. That's when feminists began waving the flag of liberation. Before then, American families lived differently. They owned one car, one television, and one stereo. Their houses averaged two thousand square feet; their children shared bedrooms; and a typical vacation might include camping. Then American women joined the workforce, and their incomes slowly created "a new norm."[13]

Today, the average home has 38 percent more square footage; kids have their own rooms; each member of the family owns his own cell phone and iPod; televisions are in many rooms;

toys abound; and a trip to Disney World is considered a rite of passage. How did this happen? Employed mothers *caused* a dramatic change in lifestyle. Families can afford posh lifestyles *because* both parents are producing an income. "The mass affluence has been driven in large part by women's incomes."[14] Therefore, to say dual-income families are a necessity is misleading. Parents are working to support the lifestyle to which they've become accustomed.

And this lifestyle can be counterproductive. Indeed, the mass movement of mothers from the home to the workplace has created an economic gerbil machine. For the average family in America, it *costs* to have both parents working full-time. Unless the wife's salary is six figures, a second income is eaten up by day care costs, commuting costs, eating out, work attire, dry cleaning, convenience foods, and, of course, taxes. Add it all up, and there isn't much left. In 1997, the Census Bureau reported that of families with children under eighteen, the *difference in the median income level* in which both the husband and wife work full-time and year-round, and families in which only one spouse was employed, was $17,638. After subtracting taxes and work-related costs, the average two-income family in America nets maybe several thousand dollars a year more than the one-income family. More often than not, mothers who join the workforce full-time do not boost a family's wealth.

No matter, economists and tax collectors cheer this phenomenon. In an article about the current recession, Megan McArdle explains that when mothers take jobs outside the home, it boosts the GDP. "She will have to pay for child care. She may need to buy new work clothes. Money will be spent on commuting, and the family will probably shift away from homemade meals to costlier prepared foods. All these transactions further swell the national income accounts."[15]

The truth is that we haven't put our wealth in perspective—

that's why we refer to mothers at home as lucky. The alternative is to believe many women live without abundance. Yet this is precisely what most families do. Most parents of non-school-age children *are* their children's primary caregivers, and they do things many families wouldn't even consider, such as live without three or more flat-screen televisions. Or cook all their meals at home. Or avoid the dry cleaner. Or take their lunch to work. Or make coffee instead of going to Starbucks. Or keep the same car for ten years. Or check out books and DVDs from the library. Or not buy their kids a lot of toys they'll never use. Or go on only one vacation a year—if that. Or live in a smaller house. Or have simple birthday parties at home. Or buy clothes they need rather than clothes they want. Or clean their homes themselves. Or cut their kids' hair themselves. Or cancel their gym membership and go running instead.

To the modern generation, this constitutes sacrifice. To previous generations, it was just life—and one that allowed mothers to be at home. "The economic necessity argument hits home with a nice solid thunk. Yet ultimately it makes no sense: as a nation we used to be a lot poorer, and women used to stay home," wrote David Gelernter.[16]

A mother's income *can*, however, become advantageous once her children are in school—even the "oppressed" women of the 1950s figured that out. After spending years at home being thrifty, the addition of a part-time job can be a boon for many families. It can even mean the difference between going on a vacation or not. A married, at-home mother's contribution to society goes far beyond her investment in child rearing (though this in itself is a huge asset to society). When mothers leave home and head to the office, it represents a loss of what economists call "utility," or what we think of as communal happiness. We know instinctively that money does not buy happiness. New research has even proven that once people reach the median level of income, there is no correlation between happiness and the amount of money we make.

It is also worth noting that the so-called need for a family to have two incomes was *not* the original purpose of the feminist push to get women out of their "comfortable concentration camp" (Betty Friedan's phrase) and into the marketplace. Women on the left were motivated by ideological, not economic, reasons. First, they wanted to achieve independence from men. Second, they wanted to eliminate the full-time homemaker from society. Their purpose was not equality or opportunity for women in the marketplace. Feminists simply wanted to make marriage and motherhood unchic. "A crucial weapon in feminism's arsenal has been the status degradation of the housewife's role," wrote Carolyn Graglia in *Domestic Tranquility*. "It is not financial need which leads the women's movement to endorse government-funded child care, but its firm belief that a woman's proper place is in the workforce."[17]

But why? Wouldn't women seeking high-powered careers be glad to enjoy less competition from other women? Not if you understand feminist ideology. Feminists realize all too well that they can never achieve a level playing field in the marketplace so long as their male competitors have the advantage of homemaker wives. "Studies show that men at the top are more likely than their colleagues to have a stay-at-home wife," wrote Web consultant and blogger Katrina Alcorn. "Could this be why today's workplace is so out of sync with today's workers?"[18]

Women on the left know that in order to get ahead more easily, they must deprive men of their advantage in having stay-at-home wives. The desire to eliminate the full-time homemaker has been feminists' goal all along.

The need for a second income was never the goal.

SEQUENCING

If multitasking is impossible, and most married mothers don't *have* to work, then what is the answer for women? That they devote themselves to their families and do nothing else with their lives? That is the question most often asked. It is also the most frustrating aspect of the working mother debate, for it frames the issue in terms of all or nothing: women either "go to work" or "stay home." To make a case for working motherhood, the media harp on the statistic that "70 percent of mothers are now in the workforce," making those who choose not to be employed feel, well, stupid. Here are the real facts about American mothers.

Approximately 60 percent of mothers with children under eighteen are their children's primary caregivers—aka "at-home moms." Twenty-six percent of these mothers are not employed, and 34 percent are employed part-time. But the Department of Labor defines a "working mother" as someone who brings home even *one dollar a year*. Also, the Labor Department doesn't delineate between mothers of babies and toddlers and mothers whose children are in school.

There's more. For non-school-age children—babies and toddlers—the percentage of mothers at home increases. Approximately 63 percent of mothers with children under age six are their children's primary caregivers. There are also approximately 148,000 stay-at-home dads in America. Bottom line: most parents take full-time, or almost full-time, care of their own children.

But you won't get these facts from the media—all they ever say is that "70 percent of mothers are in the workforce" to make you think *their* lives represent the norm. But more than half of the mothers in the American workforce work part-time (and many of them have older children). So the real number of America's "working mothers"—women who return to work immediately following their maternity leave and place their children in substitute care—is only about 35 percent! The distinction between these two groups cannot be overstated, for it often means the difference between children who are raised in their own homes by their own parents and those who are raised in day care or by a nanny.

The research is clear: most women say ideally they want to work part-time—and not at all when their children are young. According to the most recent data from the Pew Research Center, a mere 21 percent of employed mothers say full-time work is ideal. Moreover, the opinions of mothers who have chosen to stay home have changed dramatically in the past ten years. Today, a mere 16 percent say their ideal situation would be to work full-time outside the home, which is *down* from 24 percent who felt that way in 1997. What's more, nearly half of all full-time homemakers say *not* working at all outside the home is the ideal situation. In 1997, 39 percent felt this way.

Given that most women in America want to stay home with their children (and/or work part-time), young women need practical advice on how to create lives in which their needs can be met *along with their families' needs*. They don't receive that guidance. They hear only from the minority of women whose goals are in direct opposition to their own. That makes no sense.

So what *is* the answer for women? Sequencing.

"Sequencing" is a term coined by Arlene Ross Cardoza in her book of the same name. When women sequence their lives, or plan for the various seasons of a woman's life, they make space for both work and family. The most important aspect of sequencing is planning ahead—while still in college—by giving motherhood *at least as much* thought and consideration as one's career. Women in college should assume the exact opposite of what they are currently taught by professors and peers. They should assume they probably *will* want to stay home with their children, and thus will be out of the workforce for a period of time—perhaps up to ten years, depending on the number of children they have.

There are several components to planning ahead. First, women need to make a smart career choice. The inconvenient truth is that many careers do not offer women the flexibility they want. If you plan to be a doctor, lawyer, or business executive, your family life will suffer—period. The men and women who pursued these goals have paid a big price for their achievement in the long hours they must commit to their careers. This has proven to be *not* the life most women want.

Second, it is important that women plan to live near their families of origin once they have children. Though it's hard to imagine beforehand, the fact remains that women need help when their babies arrive. Millions of mothers today are exasperated because no one is around to help or counsel them. Full-time motherhood is a job that needs the help and support of family. Some can substitute with friends, and some women have enough money to pay for babysitters and nannies. But most do not—and when women don't get the help they need, their marriages suffer, which means their children suffer. One of the reasons mothers in previous generations were not as overwhelmed with motherhood as women are today is because they had Grandma around to help, as well as other moms in the neighborhood. This can make the difference between enjoying motherhood and resenting it.

The third requirement of sequencing is for women (and men) not to "live it up" before they get married. One of the reasons people believe families need two incomes today is that parents get used to a nice lifestyle prior to having children.

In previous generations, men and women married *before* they built up their careers, which helped alleviate the blow today's couples face in having to lower their standard of living after they become parents. The significance of this phenomenon should not be underestimated. It is much, much harder to climb down the ladder once you've enjoyed the good life.

The final requirement of sequencing is for women to choose a husband who works full-time at a job adequate to meet the family's needs. Modern women have failed in this mission. "The average guy believes most gals are only looking for money, but the truth is too few of us are interested in their income at all," wrote Daniela Drake and Elizabeth Ford in *Smart Girls Marry Money*.[19] Disregarding a man's work ethic and work prospects means women may be forced to remain in the workforce to keep the family afloat—and many will come to regret this. Not only will they be resentful toward their husbands; they will not enjoy the time they have with their children when they are young.

The notion of sequencing is as relevant today as it was when Ms. Cardoza's book was first released in 1986. That's because it works.

THE TRUTH ABOUT SHARED PARENTING

It takes a good dose of realism and humility for women to accept the truth about sequencing. But as *Smart Girls Marry Money* demonstrates, women have blindly accepted feminist assumptions and myths about love and marriage. The Drake-Ford book provoked much conversation when it debuted in 2009. From essays in the *Wall Street Journal* to debates in the blogosphere, women weighed in on the book's message. The general response seemed to be: "Why didn't anyone tell me this stuff? Why didn't *my mother* tell me?"

No one told them because most baby boomers are feminists, not conservatives. Even if they are conservative, they still accepted the feminist myth that women should never depend on a man. That was the common theme in the households of today's generation of parents. As a result, girls grew up assuming they would marry their best friend, both take a job, and both share in the duties at home (probably fifty-fifty). They didn't anticipate that once they became mothers, *they* would be the psychological parent—the one who always feels a direct personal responsibility for the whereabouts and well-being of each child. If and when women make these feelings public, the culture assures them they only feel this way because of outdated stereotypes. It was never imagined that women feel this way due to gender differences.

Shared parenting sounds great at face value, but it rarely works. As feminists love to point out, women continue to assume the lion's share of child care duties. What they don't tell you is why: for most women, the maternal tuning in never turns off. Feminists want you to believe that the reason household duties aren't split fifty-fifty is because men are Neanderthals, but that is bogus. Today's husbands perform about a third of the household labor. It is also common to see fathers toting their babies around in Snuglies or doing the grocery shopping with several kids in tow.

The reality is that biological differences between men and women mean some tasks are easier for, or of more interest to, a particular sex. A 2008 Gallup poll found that, even today, married couples maintain a strong and traditional division of labor—with 68 percent of married adults saying the wife does the laundry and 57 percent saying the husband does the yard work. Men also keep the car in running condition and make investment decisions (along with a myriad of other things that are often overlooked, such as taking out the trash, cleaning out the gutters, mowing the lawn, painting, cleaning the filters, moving furniture, and lifting heavy items), while women do more of the grocery shopping, meal preparation, child care, and housecleaning.

It is true that a wife's household duties are more time intensive than a husband's, but it's important to compare apples to apples. The notion that most women work the equivalent of two full-time jobs while men work only one job is a feminist fairy tale. The average woman works only twenty-six hours per week outside the home, while the average man works forty-eight hours. In other words, women have fewer obligations outside the home. Both spouses are working equally hard— just in different locales. A study in the *Journal of Economic Literature* reports that while women perform roughly seventeen more hours of work inside the home, men perform roughly twenty-two more hours outside the home. When comparing the total amount of work men and women each do *inside and outside the home*, women average fifty-six hours and men average sixty-one hours.

Many Americans are under the impression that gender role reversal—getting dads more involved at home and moms more involved at work—is always a good thing, but new research demonstrates otherwise. In *Nutureshock: New Thinking about Children*, Po Bronson and Ashley Merryman argue that many of modern society's parenting strategies are backfiring. One of the strategies they discuss is gender role reversal. In comparing progressive dads—defined as dads who share responsibility for the children and play more with their kids—to traditional dads, Dr. Sarah Schoppe-Sullivan found progressive dads had *poorer* marital quality and rated their family functioning *lower* than the fathers of couples who took traditional roles. Schoppe-Sullivan deduced that the progressive dads' greater involvement at home may have led to increased conflict over parenting practices.

That may be because a family cannot be run by a committee. The committee system neutralizes a family with continuing controversy. Simply put, parents fight a lot over who's doing more—and why one should be expected to do more than the other.

That is not to say some form of role reversal can't work. Like a mother's choice to work part-time or full-time, it doesn't have to be all-or-nothing. Gender differences simply constitute a framework that, if adhered to, makes life easier.

POLITICALLY INCORRECT FACTS
ABOUT DAY CARE

The most important aspect of sequencing requires that young people have a firm grasp of children's needs. This is yet another area in which modern women have been gypped. Women today have been raised in a work-oriented culture, one that caters to the needs of adults, not children. Feminist bias keeps women (and men) from learning the facts about children that will help young people in their quest to build happy lives. It is imperative that couples be taught *before they settle down* that children have needs that are "irreducible," say the nation's premier child psychologists Dr. Stanley Greenspan and T. Berry Brazleton. Children are not short adults—yet that is what the modern generation has been taught to believe.

They are under the impression, for example, that day care is harmless or even good for kids, which results in many couples, once they become parents, outsourcing their responsibility to substitute caregivers. According to the Pew Research Center (2009), 72 percent of Americans say "too many children are being raised in day care centers these days."[20] Indeed, many parents refuse to connect the dots between routine day care and the physical and emotional well-being of children. Instead, they allow themselves to be swayed by the feminist elite.

The biggest problem with day care in this country is that the media do not relay the facts to the American public. It isn't the mere existence of day care that's bad—it's the number of hours children spend there. The most comprehensive study to date (which we discuss further in the next chapter) shows an undeniable link between long hours in day care and increased behavioral problems in young children.

According to the *Wall Street Journal's* twenty-nine states in America—along with a few cities—now offer *mental health services* to three- and four-year-olds. "From 9.5 percent to 14.2 percent of children under six have emotional problems serious enough to hurt their ability to function, including anxiety or behavioral disorders," wrote Sue Shellenbarger, creator of the *Wall Street Journal's* Work and Family column.[21] Another study by the Archives of General Psychiatry found depression in children "as young as three." Lynn Hopson, executive director of a New Haven, Connecticut, preschool says, "We're seeing more and more children with challenging behaviors every year."[22]

In learning about the new mental health trend, Shellenbarger responded, "The idea of assigning mental health workers to child care centers and preschools is jarring; I was skeptical when I first heard the idea. Children so small shouldn't need mental-health help."[23] While she was initially shocked, Shellenbarger went on to say that she was convinced that mental-health programs benefit "entire classrooms of children by reducing behavior problems and supporting overburdened teachers."[24] Maybe they sometimes do. But it's a mistake to believe that's all there is to it. Children are masterful at hiding their true identities. Just because they comply doesn't mean the problem is solved.

Day care is an issue like divorce. Since the 1970s, Americans have chosen to believe it's better for children if their unhappily married parents divorce. Similarly, it is commonly believed that children whose mothers are unhappy at home are better off in day care. But Judith Wallerstein's twenty-five-year landmark study about children of divorce, which she chronicles in her book, *The Unexpected Legacy of Divorce*, proves it isn't that simple. Yes, children will adapt to their circumstances—they have no choice—but the effects of divorce often become shrouded behind subsequent negative behaviors or depression. Interestingly, almost every point Wallerstein makes about America's divorce culture can be applied to the day care culture.

"We embarked on a gigantic social experiment without any idea about how the next generation would be affected," she wrote. "If the truth be told, and if we are able to face it, the history of divorce in our society is replete with unwarranted assumptions that adults have made about children simply because such assumptions are congenial to adult needs and wishes."[25]

According to Shellenbarger's article in the *Wall Street Journal*, the purpose of having mental-health specialists in preschools is, among other things, to provide guidance to teachers on ways to interact with children. But it's not preschool teachers who need help in learning how to deal with children. It's parents. Parents are the folks who need an education in what children need, and we can start by telling them that too much day care is harmful.

The emotional well-being of our youngest citizens has been at stake for several decades. If, like President Obama, you believe America should "invest in early childhood education by dramatically expanding programs to ensure all of our young children are ready to enter kindergarten," that means you believe that the more exposure children have to day care and preschool, the smarter and better socialized they will be.[26]

If, on the other hand, you know instinctively, or from the plethora of research now available—or from experience—that it is children's *emotional* development that matters during the early years, you will agree with the critics of these new mental-health programs. As Lisa Snell, education director for the Reason Foundation, says, "Negative behavior in general seems to be an unintended consequence of every child going to preschool at younger and younger ages."[27]

It is essential that young couples understand the importance of children's early years. This is the time when human beings develop intangible traits such as empathy, trust, confidence, and love. The best *and only* way for children to develop these traits is for them to spend the bulk of their waking hours with a parent. As Diane Fisher, PhD, who testified to Congress in 1997 about the implications of early day care, said, "Science cannot quantify important social qualities such as compassion, courage, character, and moral vision. These traits are inextricably linked with attachment and emotional development. Do we really believe these values can be reduced to learning objectives and effectively taught in all-day early childhood group settings?"[28]

The notion that very young children require formal instruction—as President Obama claims—is patently false, and shows a marked ignorance on the part of those who make this argument. It is true that children from low-income families—whose parents may be divorced, unmarried, addicted to drugs, unemployed, or who don't know their father—can benefit from high-quality day care ("high quality" being the operative phrase); but to suggest this same theory applies to middle-class families is false.

If we spent half the amount of time, money, and energy trying to strengthen the American family as we spend on day care—and mental-health programs to fix the problems brought on by day care—America would be a much stronger nation.

· 6 ·

PANDERING TO THE FEMALE
LEFT—AT YOUR EXPENSE

*The solution lies in the rejection of politics as a solution
to one's personal problems.*

— Danielle Crittenden

The biggest chasm between feminists and conservatives is
that feminists are pro-government and conservatives are
not. Feminists do a lot of talking about wanting women's independence and empowerment, but their policies simply transfer
women's dependence on men to dependence on Uncle Sam.

One might assume these two views of government—feminist
or conservative—would divide Democrats and Republicans.
But the pervasive power feminists wield in our culture is such
that Republicans don't realize they, too, have internalized feminist assumptions and vocabulary. Americans are left with the
impression that if *Republicans* are on board (as they were with
the 1970s Equal Rights Amendment), feminist policies must
be reasonable. People don't realize they're being seduced with
their own money to support feminist goals—or if they do, they
assume the policies must be good ones.

The usual procedure of those on the left is to highlight a
victim group in order to appeal to Americans' emotions, devise

a government-financed plan to help the disadvantaged group, pretend the plan is a benefit for society, and give it sympathetic labeling.

Day Care Is for Parents, Not Children

The feminist agenda is not only anti-men and anti-marriage; it is also anti-motherhood. When feminists talk about discrimination against women in a patriarchal society, one of their examples of oppression is that mothers are expected to care for their own children. Feminists demand that this duty be taken over by the government.

In the past, husbands and fathers provided the financial support for wives and children. In prefeminist times, the laws of all fifty states made it the obligation of the husband to provide the financial support for his wife and children.

But feminists have carried on a long-running campaign to move mothers out of the home and into the labor force, and then demand that the government provide day care. There is nothing new about these goals. The demand for universal day care was one of the feminists' four hot-button resolutions passed at the International Women's Year Conference in Houston in 1977.

This goal is reiterated every year at the National Education Association's national conventions via resolutions that endorse "early childhood education programs in the public schools for children from birth through age eight."[1] The NEA annually repeats its demands:

Early childhood education programs should include a full continuum of services for parents/guardians and children, including child-care, child development, developmentally appropriate and diversity-based curricula, special education, and appropriate bias-free screening devices. The Association believes that federal legislation should be enacted to assist in organizing the implementation of fully funded early childhood education programs offered through the public schools. These programs must be available to all children on an equal basis and should include mandatory kindergarten with compulsory attendance.[2]

Hillary Clinton chimed in with the 2006 reissue of her ten-year-old book, *It Takes a Village*. (The concept of the village raising a child is a feminist dream because "village" is a liberal code word for government.) Then, in 2009, President Barack Obama pledged to spend $10 billion more per year on early childhood education (which includes day care), and his 2010 budget makes a $2 billion down payment on this commitment.

Even in 2010, feminist Gail Collins (former *New York Times* editorial page editor) gave a lengthy rant on C-SPAN2 against President Richard Nixon because he vetoed the 1971 bill proposed by Senator Walter Mondale to make federal day care for preschool children a new middle-class entitlement. But Nixon's veto message was a good one: it highlights the importance of children being raised by their own parents. His veto was, and still is, popular with the majority of Americans who believe children today spend too much time in day care.

The left also wants to diminish the role and authority parents have over their preschool children. The lingo used for this goal varies. Sometimes it's called "pre-kindergarten (pre-K)," sometimes "early childhood education," sometimes "full-day kindergarten," and sometimes just "day care." Except for old-fashioned nursery schools, which children attend for a few hours a day, two or three days a week, these programs are really euphemisms for babysitting.

They do not benefit children. The real purpose of these programs is to assist in eliminating the so-called oppression of women for being expected to care for their own babies. No research justifies center-based care for young children. The studies cited by its advocates have not been peer reviewed or replicated and are easily refuted. Pre-K center care, even so-called high-quality care, has little or no effect on children's intellectual development or school performance. On the other hand, children in day care programs seem to have more behavior problems than those who are not put in day care. But Americans never hear about that—as we learned in the last chapter.

Despite the widespread use of day care and the intense propaganda on its behalf, parents know it isn't good for children. Surveys of parents report that the majority of parents believe one parent staying at home is better than even so-called quality day care. For many years, Dr. Benjamin Spock maintained that day care is "not good for infants." Unfortunately, in the 1990s he dropped that good advice because it made employed mothers feel guilty—which he later admitted was "a cowardly thing" to do.

Fortunately, other Americans have been more courageous. Dr. Burton White, former director of the Harvard Preschool Project and one of the nation's authorities on the care of babies wrote, "After more than 30 years of research on how children develop well, I would not think of putting an infant or toddler of my own into any substitute-care program on a full-time basis, especially a center-based program."[3] And Brian Robertson, author of *Day Care Deception*, presents overwhelming evidence of the risks of putting children in day care and describes the way the media and universities have covered up evidence of those risks.

Authors William and Wendy Dreskin, who used to own a day care center, also highlight the risks in their book *The Day*

Care Decision. The most comprehensive daycare research to date, compiled by the National Institute of Child Health and Development, supports their analysis: that long hours in day-care can produce stress and behavior problems in children.

Preschool children don't need academic instruction, so the argument for it is spurious. In fact, a significant body of research shows that formal early education can actually be detrimental to children. David Elkind, professor of child development at Tufts University and author of numerous books on cognitive and social development in children and adolescents, explains that children who receive academic instruction too early are often put at risk but have no apparent gain. By attempting to teach the right things at the wrong time, early instruction can permanently damage a child's self-esteem, reduce a child's natural eagerness to learn, and block a child's natural gifts and talents. "There is no evidence that such early instruction has lasting benefits, and considerable evidence that it can do lasting harm. . . . If we do not wake up to the potential danger of these harmful practices, we may do serious damage to a large segment of the next generation," he wrote.[4]

Women on the left will never accept these truths, because day care is essential to their agenda. Without a place to house the children, feminists cannot push American women to leave their homes in search of greener pastures. And since most women lack the money to hire full-time nannies, they need to be given tax-funded day care in order to follow feminists' advice.

Leslie Bennetts, author of *The Feminine Mistake* (in which she chastises women who make the "willfully retrograde choice" to stay home with their children), is an outspoken advocate of day care. In an article for *Parade* magazine, she wrote, "The evidence is growing that quality care can have far-reaching social and educational benefits for children."[5] This is patently false—the "research" she uses to try to substantiate her claim comes from a senior vice-president for the Federal Reserve Bank of Minneapolis.

The gist of Bennetts's article is day care's affordability (or lack thereof), and she quotes Ellen Bravo, author of *Taking on the Big Boys: Why Feminism Is Good for Families, Business, and the Nation,* to support her argument. "Investing in child care will help improve the school-readiness and work-preparedness of children. We know the issue about child care isn't whether it's better or worse for kids—the quality of care is what's determinative," wrote Bravo.[6]

Actually, the research proves just the opposite: it's the *quantity* of care that matters. The number of hours children spend in day care is the determining factor. A child could be in the best possible day care environment—but if he's away from his mother for long periods of time, the damage is done. "America suffers a growing national epidemic of parental absence and disconnection. 'Quality' in day care cannot solve the problem. It doesn't even address it," wrote psychologist Diane Fisher, Ph.D., noted expert on child brain development.[7]

Dr. Stanley Greenspan, another recognized child development expert, agrees. He points out that America has struggled for years to improve day care—to no avail. The only way it can be improved, he says, is for parents to provide most of the care for their own children. Indeed, the greatest problem with day care is that too many people use it. There are simply not enough intelligent, devoted women who are willing to serve as surrogate mothers. That's one of the reasons the turnover rate in day care centers is so high—and *that* has life-altering consequences for young children. A child's greatest fear, says Greenspan, is the loss of a primary relationship.

John Bowlby, the only psychiatrist who twice received the American Psychiatric Association's highest award, warned that "a home must be very bad before it is bettered by a good institution."[8] All these experts have spent copious amounts of time with young children. Feminists claim the real problem is lack of funds. For liberals, money is always the answer. But no amount of money in the world can make up for parental absence. It's one of life's harshest realities.

SEEKING EQUAL PAY FOR UNEQUAL WORK

"Even in 2010, women make only seventy-seven cents for every dollar men earn. In my State of the Union Address, I promised to crack down on violations of equal pay laws. Today, I encourage the Senate to pass the Paycheck Fairness Act, a common-sense bill that will help ensure that men and women who do equal work receive the equal pay that they and their families deserve. I hope Congress will act swiftly so that I can sign it into law," said President Obama in a White House statement.[9]

In fact, equal pay for equal work has been U.S. law since 1963, so there's nothing new about the law or its enforcement by the Equal Employment Opportunity Commission (EEOC). Obama's statement is a throwaway line to promote the feminist myth that women are victims of employment discrimination. The seventy-seven cents mantra is a phony figure because it has no relation to how much work is performed. A long list of reasons explains why women, on average, work less in the paid labor force and therefore earn less money—such as spending years caring for their children, taking jobs that require fewer hours per week, and refusing to take the dangerous and unpleasant jobs that men take to support their families. People who work more hours, or work at more difficult, unpleasant, or risky jobs, earn more—and they should.

If what President Obama said were really true—that businesses get away with paying women less than men for the same work—then bosses would hire only or mostly women! Stating that women in America earn less than men, without explaining why, either shows a marked ignorance on the president's part or demonstrates his willingness to lie to the American people.

The pay gap in America is not between men and women at all, but between married women and other men and women who spend their lifetimes in the workforce. It is primarily the result of a voluntary domestic division of labor, not discrimination by a conspiracy of male chauvinists. Women who remain single and childless, stay in the labor force, and work long hours earn about as much as men.

Married men with children earn the most, while married women with children earn the least. As the number of children increases, a married man spends more hours in the workforce to support his family, and a married woman spends fewer hours. There will never be male-female pay parity so long as most women spend part of their lives caring for their children. The proper role of government is to provide equal opportunity, not preferential treatment. In America, each of us is paid a compromise between what we want and what someone is willing to pay. Those millions of decisions add up to what we call the private enterprise system.

The feminists' concept of government wage control began in the 1980s when they invented a theory called Comparable Worth. Its proponents want to force businesses to pay wages based on worth, not work. This is absurd—almost everyone thinks he is worth more than he is being paid! Unable to sell this notion to any legislature, feminists do what liberals always do: they run to the judiciary to find activist judges to force employers to order pay raises and promotions to women.

The concept of comparable worth is that some commissar (or czarina) of wages should use the power of government to make the wages of jobs held traditionally by women (such as office clerks) equal to the wages of groups of jobs held traditionally by men (such as construction workers). Which jobs get raises and how much, and which get pay cuts and how much, would be within the subjective and arbitrary discretion of feminist bureaucrats.

President Obama and his feminist cohorts might get a reality check if they read Dr. Warren Farrell's book *Why Men Earn More: The Startling Truth Behind the Pay Gap and What Women Can Do About It.* Dr. Farrell provides massive documentation to explain why men earn more than women. It's because men work more hours per week, take more hazardous jobs, work at less desirable locations, under less pleasant working conditions, and take more technical training than women. Men suffer 92 percent of all occupational deaths because they are willing to work at the most hazardous occupations, such as firefighting, construction, and mining.

Dr. Farrell points out that women's career choices usually involve a balance between work and the rest of life. Women are more likely to balance income with a desire for safety, fulfillment, potential for personal growth, flexibility, and proximity to home. When you select the type of job you apply for and train yourself to take, there are trade-offs. Most women happily trade career advancement for more family time.

In his first week in office, President Obama signed the Lilly Ledbetter Act, which eliminated the statute of limitations on discrimination claims so that a worker can sue in federal court for alleged pay discrimination that supposedly happened twenty or more years earlier. This law exposes businesses to vast new liabilities extending back many years. It's impossible to refute lies about discrimination that date back decades if bosses and witnesses are no longer around to defend themselves.

Lilly Ledbetter worked for Goodyear for nineteen years and retired with benefits. She then suddenly claimed that her supervisor, long dead, had committed gender discrimination against her many years earlier. The jury awarded Lilly $3.5 million. Imagine what this kind of verdict does to a company struggling to compete with foreign manufacturers who are not subject to feminist nonsense. Goodyear appealed and won in the U.S. Supreme Court, but the president, pandering to feminists, signed the Lilly Ledbetter Law to overturn the Court's decision.

There's more. When President Obama announced his multibillion-dollar stimulus bill, he promised it would create millions of "shovel-ready" jobs. This conjured up images of crews in hard hats repairing our nation's infrastructure, bridges, and highways. But feminists swung into action with accusations that the stimulus discriminated against women because its jobs would go mostly to men. Feminists had no sympathy for the men who were the victims of two-thirds of the eleven million jobs lost since the recession began in 2007, so feminists demanded a meeting where they lectured Obama's economic advisers and hurled their demands that the stimulus package create jobs that women like—such as comfortable inside jobs with air-conditioning and carpeted floors.

To intimidate administration officials, they insisted that participants in the meeting be seated in a circle without a table between them, a format that enabled the feminists to be particularly confrontational. The feminists created their own vocabulary to shout at the men—"human infrastructure" and "human bridges"—which are code words for social service, health care, day care, and government jobs.

With the compliance of Nancy Pelosi and Harry Reid, feminists succeeded in getting the majority of stimulus jobs—and Obama signed the revised bill. A member of Pelosi's staff dared to offer the suggestion that "apron ready" could be the female equivalent of the term "shovel ready," but feminists didn't think that was funny. (Feminists have no sense of humor, you know. They're too busy being angry, which uses up most of their energy.)

When President Obama presented his multi-trillion-dollar budget, he declared he was calling for a freeze in discretionary spending. Feminists immediately had a tantrum and won exemption from the freeze for all feminist programs and organizations. Instead, they will get what White House spokeswoman Kate Bedingfield admitted are "significant funding increases."[10]

A White House document titled "Opportunity and Progress for Women and Girls" describes fifteen federal programs that will receive increased funding to appease the female left. The Violence Against Women project, for example, is targeted for a 22 percent increase. The budget would also appropriate $50 million to give grants to incentivize the states to adopt paid family leave and increase funding for day care, with Head Start scheduled for additional funding of nearly $1 billion. Obama's budget also increases funding for a new program to recruit under-graduate students from underrepresented groups in science and technology careers and increases funding for a special program to give women more jobs in academic science and engineering careers.

Diana Furchtgott-Roth, a senior fellow at the Hudson Institute, exposed more of Obama's pandering to the feminists in the Dodd-Frank financial regulation bill, passed by Congress in 2010. Section 342 sets up at least twenty Offices of Minority and Women Inclusion—separate offices in the Treasury, the Federal Deposit Insurance Corporation, the Federal Housing Finance Agency, the twelve Federal Reserve regional banks, the Board of Governors of the Fed, the National Credit Union Administration, the Comptroller of the Currency, the Securities and Exchange Commission, and the Consumer Financial Protection Bureau. Each office will have its own director and staff to promote gender diversity and the "fair inclusion" of women not only in its own agency but also in the workforces of its contractors and subcontractors. This is a significant change in our employment law because *it mandates gender and racial quotas.* The institutions will be able to show compliance and avoid lawsuits only by imposing quotas on their workforce.

THE POLITICS OF MARRIAGE

That 70 percent of unmarried women voted for Barack Obama in the 2008 presidential election tells you most of what you need to know about the feminists' goals and their political allies. For years, women on the left have worked to push wives into the workforce and make husbands and fathers irrelevant. Chief feminist Ruth Bader Ginsburg complained in her 1977 tax-funded book, *Sex Bias in the U.S. Code,* that "the adult world is (and should be) divided into two classes—independent men, whose primary responsibility is to win bread for a family, and dependent women, whose primary responsibility is to care for children and household. This concept must be eliminated."[11]

The politics are obvious. Without a husband, single moms look to Big Brother government as provider of their living expenses. And since Democrats can always outbid Republicans in big-spending programs, an increase in the number of single moms means more women voting for the Democrats. Since Obama was elected, Democrats have worked to increase the number of single moms by boosting the flow of taxpayer-paid incentives to subsidize the non-marriage lifestyle. A marriage penalty of more than $2,000 was built into Obama's health care act. That's the additional cost of health insurance if a cohabitating couple decides to marry.

When a *Wall Street Journal* reporter quizzed the Democrat authors of ObamaCare, they made it clear that this differential was deliberate. The staffer justified discriminating against marriage because "you have to decide what your goals are." Democrats certainly are not going to allow traditional marriage to be preferred over couples who shack up! To the Democrats, both scenarios are acceptable, but the non-married lifestyle is politically preferable because it produces more votes for Democrats.

The congressional battle over ObamaCare also illustrates how feminists are determined to keep abortion as the number-one women's right and force taxpayers to pay for as many abortions as they can. In the *Daily Beast*, feminist author and former Women's Studies professor Linda Hirshman makes it clear that support for abortion rights is the litmus tests for true feminism. Ruth Bader Ginsburg has complained for years about the Supreme Court decision in *Harris v. McRae*, which ruled that the Constitution does not require the taxpayers to pay for abortions. Nevertheless, feminists use every legislative and judicial opportunity to try to make the taxpayers finance abortions.

Barack Obama was always enthusiastic about these feminist goals. Campaigning for president on July 9, 2008, he told Planned Parenthood, "The first thing I'd do as president is sign the Freedom of Choice Act. That's the first thing I'd do."[12] Fortunately, Congress didn't give him the chance to sign FOCA, which would nullify all restrictions on abortion—including the Partial-Birth Abortion Ban Act, the Hyde Amendment, parental consent laws, and informed consent laws.

Obama and his feminist groupies went all out to include abortion funding in his health care act, and their persistence almost derailed the bill. Just before final passage, abortion funding was retained in the bill when a handful of Democrats betrayed their pro-life promises, pretending that an Obama executive order could override the federal law's language requiring insurance companies to cover abortion services.

Single moms are a major target of the female left. The goal is to increase the number of single moms by increasing the flow of taxpayer-paid incentives that subsidize the non-marriage lifestyle. The left expects this plan to lock in single moms' dependence on government and allegiance to the Democratic Party. They respect Ronald Reagan's maxim that goes something like this: If we subsidize something, we'll get more of it; if we tax it, we'll get less of it.

Welfare as we know it was created by Lyndon B. Johnson's Great Society in the 1960s, largely as a do-good program to assist widows with young children. It was recognized even in 1965 in the famous Moynihan Report as a social disaster that resulted in millions of fatherless children, illegitimacy, and dependency on government. The fault was to channel taxpayer handouts only to mothers, thereby providing a powerful financial incentive for fathers to depart; they were not needed anymore.

The Personal Responsibility and Work Opportunity Act of 1996, known as Welfare Reform, was cheered as a big achievement of the Republican Congress and its Contract with America. That law helped to move millions of welfare recipients out of dependency and into productive jobs. However, one of the Obama administration's first acts—surprise, surprise—was to repeal that Welfare Reform. The Democratic Congress provided bonuses to states that increase their spending on Temporary Assistance for Needy Families (TANF). Democrats know who butters their bread: single moms who get their living expenses from Big Brother government.

This political strategy is also conveniently set forth in a sixty-page document called *Advancing the Economic Security of Unmarried Women*. It's published by John Podesta's left-wing think tank, the Center for American Progress, the same foundation that produced *The Shriver Report*.

The Podesta opus sets the stage for the Democrats' legislative proposals by asserting that our definition of family is an "outdated, stuck in the 1950s notion of a nuclear family that excludes too many of today's nontraditional families."[13] The Podesta document then describes eighty-three pieces of proposed congressional legislation that will funnel taxpayers' money mostly to unmarried women. You can get the flavor and the message from the alluring titles:

- The Hiring Incentives to Restore Employment (HIRE) Act would "particularly benefit" unmarried women because it would incentivize hiring in the education and health services industry.
- The Unemployment Insurance Modernization Act would require expansion in eligibility and benefits to help women.
- The Paycheck Fairness Act would "improve" the 1963 Equal Pay Act based on the falsehood that "women workers earn seventy-seven cents for every dollar a comparable man makes."
- The Employment Non-Discrimination Act (ENDA) would benefit lesbian and bisexual women.
- The Living American Wage Act and the Working for Adequate Gains for Employment in Services (WAGES) Act would improve the pay of "traditionally female jobs" in day care, early childhood education, and health care.
- The Pathways Advancing Career Training (PACT) Act and the Strengthening Employment Clusters to Organize Regional Success (SECTORS) Act would give funding to states to provide training for and access to nontraditional high-wage jobs and careers for women.
- The Family and Medical Leave Inclusion Act and the Family and Medical Leave Enhancement Act would expand the definition of family to allow unmarried partners and same-sex spouses to use the benefits of family-leave laws.

- The Family Income to Respond to Significant Transitions (FIRST) Act and the Federal Employees Paid Parental Leave (FEPPLA) Act would give women paid family leave.
- The Healthy Families Act would require employers to provide paid sick days, which the document claims would help women because "women are disproportionately affected" by not having paid sick days.
- The Domestic Violence Leave Act and the Security and Financial Empowerment (SAFE) Act would make women eligible for leave for a variety of problems connected with alleged domestic violence.
- The Starting Early, Starting Right Act would provide "high-quality" day care.
- The Right Start Child Care and Education Act, the Helping Families Afford to Work Act, and the Balancing Act are all designed to provide cash and services to single moms.
- The Earned Income Tax Credit is already worth up to $5,657 for a single parent with custody of three children. The Podesta report failed to mention that the Government Accountability Office reports that the IRS estimates that between 27 percent and 32 percent of EITC dollars are collected fraudulently.

Of course, all these eighty-three bills probably won't pass—just as Education Secretary Arne Duncan's idea to have American schools be open "fourteen hours a day, seven days a week, twelve months of the year" would never happen. But they do illustrate the politics of Obama Democrats and feminists—and their political alliance. They also demonstrate how welfare has, in the hands of government, ballooned into a spending monster to serve the left's political agenda.

· 7 ·

THE EXPENDABLE MALE

The wound that unifies all men is the wound of their disposability.

—Warren Farrell

In a *More* magazine interview, actress Mary-Louise Parker admits to liking things that are "psychologically dangerous." Ms. Parker never married, but she has two children—one from a previous relationship and one who is adopted. When asked what it's like to date as a single mom, she said a man once asked if her being a mom meant the two of them would not be able to go out alone together very much. Parker replied, "Yes, that's exactly what it means. It means you come fourth, 'cause it's my kids, my job, and my family."[1]

Welcome to twenty-first-century America.

In the span of just a few decades, American women have managed to demote men from respected providers and protectors to being unnecessary, irrelevant, and expendable. It's a wonder men marry at all. You may recall Andrea Wong's words from Chapter 1: *"There is something special that happens when you get a group of powerful women in a room . . . and shut the door.*" That is a perfect metaphor. The feminist elite would love nothing more than to shut men out.

If you think we're exaggerating, consider these elitist, condescending examples:

- Author and journalist Natalie Angier begins an article in the *New York Times* by writing, "Women may not find this surprising, but one of the most persistent and frustrating problems in evolutionary biology is the male. Specifically . . . why doesn't he just go away?"[2]

- In a CNN interview with Maureen Dowd about her 2005 book, *Are Men Necessary?* Dowd says, "Now that women don't need men to reproduce and refinance, the question is, will we keep you around? And the answer is, 'You know, we need you in the way we need ice cream—you'll be more ornamental.'"[3]

- Several years ago Katie Couric interviewed a young bride on the *Today* show who had been jilted at the altar. Jokingly, Couric asked the young woman if she'd "considered castration as an option."[4]

- Lisa Belkin, a blogger for the *New York Times* whose work is provocative but not overly biased, wrote, "We are standing at a moment in time when the role of gender is shifting seismically. At this moment an argument can be made for two separate narrative threads—the first is the retreat of men as this becomes a woman's world."[5]

- In an article in the *Atlantic* titled "Are Fathers Necessary?" author Pamela Paul wrote, "The bad news for Dad is that despite common perception, there's nothing objectively essential about his contribution."[6]

Such statements are shocking. It is *impossible* to imagine men making these same comments about women. Few men would dare to joke about women in public—they wouldn't get away with it! "I've been very careful about offending women. I'll challenge presidents any day, but taking on half the world is asking too much," wrote ABC news anchor Sam Donaldson in *Hold On, Mr. President!*[7]

It isn't just a matter of being polite. Men can lose their credibility, or even their jobs, for saying the kinds of things Angier, Dowd, Couric, Belkin, and Paul said. Even when men use *the nicest words they can think of* to describe negative behavior of a woman, they get walloped. That's what happened to Mitt Romney when he was campaigning for governor of Massachusetts in 2002. He called the histrionics of his female Democratic opponent "unbecoming," and feminists exploded in tantrums of accusations that he had used a sexist word.

The brouhaha over comments made by former Harvard University president Larry Summers is another example. In 2005, Summers suggested the underrepresentation of women in the top levels of science and engineering could be due to a "different availability of aptitude at the high end."[8] This is a true enough statement, and Summers substantiated his argument with reason, common sense, and experience. He also made two other suggestions for why he thought the discrepancy exists. But feminists didn't tolerate any of it. They couldn't get past the implication that women could have any less ability than men in science and engineering. Even when Summers apologized again and again, it did him no good. His female colleagues hammered him until he resigned.

Bart Stupak also caved in to feminist pressure. Despite the support he had from the American people who wanted him to stick to his guns, he abandoned his announced position on abortion limitations in President Obama's health care bill. Then he decided not to run again for his congressional seat in 2010.

Bill O'Reilly is one of the few powerful men who have—on occasion—taken feminists to task. Several years ago he mentioned to his guest, Fox commentator (and feminist) Margaret Hoover, that single motherhood—which stands at an alarming 41 percent—"drives poverty if you don't have a father supporting the family."[9] Hoover then charged back at O'Reilly for making what she called a "sexist" comment.

An incredulous O'Reilly asked, "It's sexist because I just told the truth? There's got to be someone else giving the mother money besides the government!"[10] At which point, Hoover—who has no children—hemmed and hawed, but ultimately conceded. "Okay, I'll give you that." Translation: It still sounds sexist, but I guess you're right. Someone has to take care of the children, and someone has to bring home the bacon.

Hoover is a good example of a supposedly conservative woman who has been completely brainwashed by feminist tutelage. Indeed, the feminist elite include Democrats *and* Republicans. These women claim they want to compete with men; but when push comes to shove, their victimhood mentality gets in the way.

When women in the media consistently portray American women as victims, a negative image of men unfolds—and the result is a society in which women think less highly of men. This pattern has morphed into the notion that women don't need men at all, which is why it has now become socially acceptable for women to create families on their own. Mothers who divorce their husbands are exalted in the media, as if single motherhood is somehow empowering.

Yet there is nothing empowering about being a single mom. Ask any *honest* single mother what it's like to raise a child on her own, and she'll concede that it's extremely difficult. Men, it turns out, really are useful. Not only are there countless household tasks husbands do, children miss their fathers. This need becomes manifestly evident the moment parents separate. And it is women—since mothers usually get custody of the kids—who must deal with the fallout.

This is not the message we glean from society. After decades of feminist influence, the choice of single motherhood has become a bona fide "right" of American women. At no other time in history could we open one of the number-one magazines in the country to find a story about a famous actress who claims marriage doesn't need to be a prerequisite for motherhood. The headline on the August 2010 cover page of *People* magazine, beneath a picture of Jennifer Aniston, reads, "I Don't Need a Man to Be a Mom." Inside, Aniston tells *People*, "Women are realizing they don't have to settle with a man just to have a child."

When her leftist views are challenged, Aniston responds, "Love is love and family is what is around you."[11] Clearly, Aniston lives in a Hollywood bubble—this assertion is both shortsighted and immature.

Perhaps Aniston's views are the reason she was all too happy to star in *The Switch*, one of three movies that were released last year (to poor reviews) about donor insemination. This film, as well as *The Kids Are All Right*, portrays children who were conceived by use of a sperm donor—a development that is hailed as empowering for women. The message of the movies is clear: children of donor fathers "turn out fine" (like children in day care supposedly do). So if women find themselves at age forty and childless, they can simply order some sperm and life will be grand.

Perhaps this works in the movies. In real life, the story is very different. Elizabeth Marquardt, Norval D. Glenn, and Karen Clark wrote a report by the Center for Marriage and Families called "My Daddy's Name is Donor." The gist of the report is that many children conceived by donor sperm grow up angry and confused. More important, adult offspring of single mothers by choice were 177 percent more likely to report having trouble with drugs and alcohol than children born to two biological parents. They were also 146 percent more likely to report having been "in trouble with the law" before age twenty-five.

If that's not a case for Dad, we don't know what is.

Unfortunately, Dad's role in society has been undermined long before he becomes a man. Feminists have been rejecting masculinity for years—and putting pressure on America's institutions to do the same. Indeed, they have waged a full-scale assault on the American male.

SCHOOLBOYS

In 2009, the magazine *Working Mother* (of all places) published an article called "The Truth about Boys and Girls." Meredith F. Small, Ph.D., highlighted the age-old wisdom that "boys will be boys" and used the latest research on gender differences to substantiate her argument. The male and female brains, she wrote, are unique from birth. A "batch of brain studies" seems to indicate what mothers have always known: generally speaking, girls are social creatures and boys are action-oriented. (But don't think the editors at *Working Mother* have awakened from their feminist slumber. Despite the theme of the article—that gender differences clearly exist—the editors chose to emphasize in big, bold letters this sentence: "It's completely natural when a little boy loves nail polish or a girl her toy truck.")

Researchers have now used MRIs of older kids' brains to explain the differences. The portion of the brain that pertains to language works harder in girls' brains than it does in boys' brains. Infant girls make a great deal of eye contact with one person and show more empathy than infant boys. Infant boys prefer moving objects, which helps to explain their subsequent interest in 3-D and moving toys, such as cars and trucks. They are also more likely to run and jump than girls, preferring active play rather than reading.

Despite such overwhelming evidence of sex differences, American boys are subjected to the feminization process as early as kindergarten. Surrounded mostly by women (and often feminists), both curriculum and activities revolve around the needs of girls and girls' interests. Assigned stories are in subjects girls like (such as fairy tales), rather than subjects boys like (such as adventure and battles). Moreover, first-grade boys are roughly nine months behind girls in coordination, yet the emphasis in this grade is on sitting still at a desk. Many schools have also eliminated recess, which does not bode well for boys. They are active by nature and need to run around, and when they can't sit still, teachers and administrators often wrongly attribute this to ADD or ADHD.

Many elementary school teachers, raised to believe in a false concept of gender equality, are reluctant to admit any gender differences between males and females. Some think little boys are just unruly girls. "Boys learn to subdue their more spirited, intrepid behavior in school, their male instincts of competition and individualism quashed in the interest of what's best for girls as they walk like lemmings over the edge of the radical feminist cliff by the time they reach high school," wrote schoolteacher and op-ed contributor Jane Gilvary for the *Bulletin* (Philadelphia) in "Skinny Jeans, John Wayne, and the Feminization of America (August 24, 2010)."

Experts believe developmentally inappropriate expectations and practices are causing normal boy behavior to be wrongly labeled as misbehavior, and normal learning patterns to be mislabeled as learning disabilities. The result is that many boys become frustrated and discouraged by school in the early grades. "Boys learn early that they belong to the 'bad' sex and their female counterparts to the 'good,'" writes Kathleen Parker in *Save the Males.*[12]

OFF TO COLLEGE: THE PERILS OF TITLE IX

When young men enter college, they come face-to-face with an anti-male attitude, augmented by the power of government. Right off the bat, college men are restricted from competing in the sports they love. Title IX is a controversial section of the Education Amendments of 1972, which is a simple, straightforward federal law requiring that schools and colleges receiving federal funds not discriminate "on the basis of sex."

This law says nothing about equal numbers of men and women, sex-integration, gender quotas, "proportionality," affirmative action, remedies for underrepresentation of past discrimination, or even sports. Title IX's author, representative Edith Green, promised the law is "exceedingly explicit so that the establishment of quotas would be prohibited."[13]

The Department of Education wrote the regulation that Title IX compliance must be demonstrated in one of three ways. One of those ways, labeled "proportionality," became a powerful weapon in the hands of feminist bureaucrats. Beginning with

Jimmy Carter's Department of Education, Title IX has been aggressively used to abolish college men's sports: wrestling, gymnastics, track and field, swimming, hockey, golf, and football. That many of these college men's teams had produced dozens of Olympic medalists doesn't matter to feminists.

Perhaps left-wing women resent it that college sports have produced many conservatives. Football gave us the late Jack Kemp, the late Supreme Court Justice Byron White, and former Congressmen Steve Largent and J. C. Watts. College wrestling programs brought us conservative stalwarts former Defense Secretary Donald Rumsfeld and former House Speaker Dennis Hastert, plus current U.S. Representative Jim Jordan, who was a state champion wrestler in two states (Wisconsin and Ohio). Track and field gave us former Congressman Jim Ryun, one of the greatest runners of all time.

Enrollment in academic courses is now approaching 60 percent women to 40 percent men, so the proportionality test means that athletic teams must enforce this same ratio. This rule is absurd because it's a fact of human nature that men are more interested than women in participating in competitive sports. It is typical for colleges to have difficulty finding enough women to meet their quota targets because some women, called "re-entry" women, are long past the age of wanting to compete on a soccer field or basketball court. But common sense and facts of human nature do not deter feminists, and colleges find that using proportionality is the only safe way to avoid lawsuits.

Title IX quotas forced the elimination of 467 college wrestling teams, a particular target of feminist anti-masculine bias. The attack on wrestling shows that Title IX is not about equalizing male-female funding, since wrestling is one of the least expensive sports. Wrestling teams have been eliminated even when completely financed by alumni and supporters, as have other men's teams that were willing to raise their own funds.

Howard University canceled wrestling and baseball on the same day. It isn't surprising that male enrollment has dropped to only 34 percent, compared to 66 percent female. After the feminist National Women's Law Center filed a complaint against Boston University over its sports programs, the university ended its football team that had been in existence for ninety-one years, and male enrollment dropped to 40 percent.

Feminist ideologues predicted the 2008 Olympic Games in China would prove women have closed the gender gap in athletic performance. Americans were told that all women need is more experience, better training, and stronger coaching (which presumably the patriarchy had denied them). But the Beijing Olympics proved women are slower in running, swimming, and cycling. Whether it is a 100-meter race on the track, a marathon, a 200-meter butterfly swim, or a 10-kilometer marathon swim, the same pattern holds: men are faster.

Of course, some women are faster than some men. A very lean, well-trained woman will be faster than a less lean, less fit man. But that's not the issue in the Olympics. Men and women are just plain different. When the U.S. Civil Rights Commission in 2010 recommended colleges use a survey to determine student interest in athletics as the "best method available" for complying with the law without requiring arbitrary gender quotas, the Obama administration—predictably—rejected that helpful suggestion, sticking to the proportionality rule that serves feminist goals.

Demanding equal participation in college sports is absurd—and it's wholly unfair to men, who are up against feminists who have an agenda and think they know best. The student newspaper at the University of Kansas ridiculed gender quotas with this spoof: "Many women may say they don't want to play sports, but after generations of patriarchal oppression, women don't really know what they want. The goal of perfectly equal gender ratios is more important than what anybody 'wants.' College sports for women should be compulsory."

FEMINIST TRAPS FOR ADULT MEN

After college, the not-yet-thoroughly emasculated male goes into the real world unprepared for the workplace as yet another feminist environment. Indeed, the workplace is a minefield for men. In an article titled "The End of Men" in *The Atlantic*, Hanna Rosin boasts that in 2010 "women became the majority of the workforce for the first time in U.S. history. Most managers are now women, too."[14] Jessica Bennett crowed in a *Newsweek* article that women will "rule the world."

Navigating feminist terrain both inside and outside the workplace has become the new challenge for men in America. The problem is that most men don't want to compete with women—it isn't natural. And taking their colleagues, girlfriends, and wives to task for their feminist beliefs is much too intimidating. Even if men disagree with feminist philosophy, they know they'll be branded a chauvinist if they speak up.

That's why trying to survive the feminist workplace is challenging—and dangerous. If a man would like to ask one of his female colleagues for a date, he must be careful. If he's her superior and his overture isn't welcome, he could be accused of sexual harassment—which is no small matter. If a woman feels uncomfortable in *any* way when a male colleague asks her out, she can claim he created a hostile environment. "Sexual initiatives by men toward women below them at work are the most frequent definition of sexual harassment. When it works, it's called courtship. When it doesn't, it's called harassment," wrote Warren Farrell in *The Myth of Male Power*.[15]

One brave judge with experience in sexual harassment cases,

Missouri judge Robert H. Dierker Jr., describes his observations in his book, *The Tyranny of Tolerance: A Sitting Judge Breaks the Code of Silence to Expose the Liberal Judicial Assault.* Judge Dierker explains that claims of sexual harassment have become a means by which feminists vent their malice toward men. He wrote that feminism's "confluence" with the left has "spawned a truly horrible jurisprudence." Feminists have determined that the law should not treat women the same as men but *better*—to compensate women for centuries of oppression. "Sexual harassment law threatens to become a weapon by which [feminists] ensure the oppression of men."[16]

Americans are largely unaware of how men are treated in courtrooms across America. Instead, we are routinely exposed to messages that sell the notion of women as harassment victims. On the *CBS Evening News*, Katie Couric solemnly warned little girls to expect sexual harassment. She reported that "90 percent of teen girls say they have been harassed at least once." And what does this harassment consist of? "Unwanted romantic attention, demeaning gender-related comments based on their appearance, and unwanted physical contact."

Feminists don't know what they want. They fight to protect themselves from their own mistakes, but then they fight for the freedom to make those mistakes. They want free sex, but they also want the ability to punish the man when they change their mind.

In addition to charges of sexual harassment and date rape on college campuses, feminists have invented a new crime called "gray rape." *Cosmopolitan* defines gray rape as "sex that falls somewhere between consent and denial and is even more confusing than date rape because often both parties are unsure of who wanted what."[17] Such fuzzy scenarios are impossible to prove in a court of law. But what's even more insidious about date rape, or gray rape, is that *men* become the victims. Inebriated women who end up having sex without meaning to can cry date rape, and the guy could end up in prison! Journalist Laura Sessions Stepp asks: "So how do you avoid being a victim without giving up the right to be sexually independent and assertive?"

Apparently no one told Ms. Stepp that the only way to avoid being a victim of gray rape is to steer clear of precarious situations in the first place. That may not eliminate rape altogether, but it would eradicate the mess of "gray rape."

Some men greet the feminist challenge by setting out to enjoy the smorgasbord of sex easily available to them—it's often too tempting to give up. But after men get tired of the playboy lifestyle, finding a suitable wife can be difficult. Matt, age forty-four, recalls his single days with a bit of angst:

> Life from my mid-twenties to late thirties can be summarized by this statement: Go out, get drunk, hit on countless unsuspecting, yet sometimes willing participants. I had a handful of serious relationships, but I knew none would ever work 'til death do us part.
>
> People often asked me, "Why didn't you marry her? Or her? Or. . . ." I always responded the same way: "Because I'm smart. I knew it wouldn't work, and I don't want to be another statistic of divorce." It got to the point, when I was thirty-seven years old or so, I truly believed I'd never get married.

Matt finally did get married—to a divorced woman with three school-age children. "To go from my single, debauchery lifestyle to married with three kids almost overnight never crossed my mind. But it's the best thing that has ever happened to me."

Why, we might ask, was an instant family the best thing that could have happened to Matt? For one thing, the chance of a forty-year-old male meeting someone closer to his age who isn't divorced, and who doesn't have children, is slim. If Matt had insisted on having children of his own, he would have had to seek out a younger woman. But many of them are not ready or willing to settle down.

Matt's feelings also make sense from a sociological perspective. Men have a need for marriage and family. When they don't marry, they often make bad choices. "Without a durable relationship with a woman, a man's sexual life is a series of brief and temporary exchanges. But with love, sex becomes refined by selectivity, and other dimensions of his personality are engaged and developed," wrote George Gilder in *Men and Marriage*.[18]

Contrary to what movies like *He's Just Not That Into You* suggest, most men do want to settle down and have children of their own. There are countless men who would be happy to do so if they did not have sex so freely available and if their girlfriends weren't so willing to cohabit. Simply put, feminism has removed the incentive for men to marry.

Yet marry many do—at their own risk.

EMASCULATED HUSBANDS

There was a time in the past (or so we're told) when wives brought slippers to their husbands when they came home from work. It was a nice gesture—if indeed women did this with any regularity—that, unfortunately, became a sign of oppression once feminists grabbed microphones to complain.

Today this scenario is completely reversed—but no one speaks of men being oppressed. In 2010, CBS Harry Smith interviewed author A. J. Jacobs and his wife. Jacobs chronicled a month in which he agreed to do everything his wife wanted him to do. During the interview, Harry Smith told Jacobs' wife—in the kindest way possible—that men already feel as if they're at the beck and call of their wives. Julie responded by cutting him off and telling him that while he may feel that way, he dismisses the fact that there are "many, many other things" wives *don't* tell their husbands to do—as if she should be commended for not being more demanding than she already is. The program then showed the couple in their home, as Jacob "services" his wife by giving her a foot rub and performs countless other tasks she had requested. Just *imagine* if that scenario was turned around. Unthinkable!

While Jacobs' story is an extreme example, it is a good analogy for what has happened to the dynamics within marriage. Contrary to feminist dogma, women have always held the power inside the home: they raised the children; they made most household decisions; they decided what to buy; and they spent their husbands' paychecks. Dad often felt like an outsider.

Yet there were two things men could count on to bolster their self-esteem: their income, which they knew was essential, and their masculine nature, which was, at the time, respected by women and society. Feminists have succeeded in taking away both those things, and men are left on unfamiliar terrain. "The feminization of fathers is rampant. And women have played no small part in this transformation," wrote Aisha Sultan in the *St. Louis Post-Dispatch*.[19]

Sultan quoted Kathleen Gerson, professor of sociology at New York University and author of *The Unfinished Revolution: How a New Generation is Reshaping Family, Work, and Gender in America*, who admits that parents today are unsure about who's supposed to do what. (See "The Truth about Shared Parenting" in Chapter 5.) Gerson says women say they want "sensitive" men who will be equal partners at home, rather than just economic providers. "But," wrote Sultan, "the hyper-nurturing dad feels too far flung in the other direction."[20]

That's because women on the left were never looking for

equality, as they claimed. They wanted to emasculate men—and now they have. Consequently, the modern generation is confused. "As women, we may love men, live with men, and bear sons, but we have yet to understand men and boys," wrote Louann Brizendine, MD, in *The Male Brain*.[21] Men don't know what women want, which is made even worse by the fact that women themselves don't know what *they* want!

This is illustrated by the popular film *The Hours*. It's a depressing tale that makes heroines out of three feminists who put their own self-fulfillment above every other goal. They betray their marital promises, abandon faithful husbands, flout moral standards, walk out on the duties of motherhood, and trample on everyone who was unfortunate enough to come into contact with them. Women on the left love this movie. They admire any woman who seeks her own identity apart from any man.

But *The Hours* proves the folly of feminist ideology. The narcissistic pursuit of personal happiness by the three female leads—Virginia Woolf, Laura, and Clarissa—produces loneliness and suicide. It's amazing feminists can't learn their own lessons.

Yet after decades of insisting on faux equality, scores of women have changed their minds. Women have started to figure out that the feminist plan doesn't work. "Today's generation is returning to the traditional values of home and family—and looking to men to be the breadwinners," wrote Beth Hale in *Mail Online*.[22]

Not only do parents struggle with gender role reversal; so do children. "Even though some modern parenting styles endorse the laid-back father as more likely to be a good dad than the high-testosterone macho man, biological research suggests the opposite may be true," wrote Brizendine.[23]

Is it possible the Marlboro man, the guy feminists insisted was so terrible, is missed?

UNILATERAL DIVORCE

If there's one thing feminists love, it's divorce—they consider it liberating (Chapter 5 offers numerous examples). Their original slogan was "liberation," which means freeing women from the shackles of marriage and the duties of motherhood. In 1969, California became the first state to adopt what was called no-fault divorce. The movement to change divorce laws swept across the country during the 1970s, the heyday of the women's liberation movement.

The more accurate label for no-fault divorce is *unilateral divorce*, for it means either spouse can break the marriage contract and walk away without any fault by the other party. Previously, getting a court to dissolve a marriage contract required a reason—some evidence of fault by the other spouse. Not anymore. Dissolving a marriage today is as simple as checking a box that reads, "See ya. I'm out of here."

Indeed, unilateral divorce introduced a new concept in America: dissolving a marriage on the ground of "irreconcilable differences." That means just about anyone can get divorced for any reason whatsoever. Is this good for some people? Perhaps. But it has come at great cost.

The argument in favor of no-fault divorce, which feminists wholeheartedly support, is that it makes unhealthy marriages easier to dissolve and diminishes the nastiness that accompanied many fault-based divorces. It also shortens the time it used to take for couples to obtain a divorce.

But there are drawbacks to unilateral divorce. First, it takes away one spouse's attempt to save the marriage. Second, it gives more power to family court judges to decide who gets custody of the children, how the marital assets will be split, and who should receive support—for when no spouse is to blame, judges' decisions are based on their own feelings. And feelings are subjective. The notion that judges, government-appointed psychologists and counselors, and bureaucrats can dictate what is in the best interest of the child rather than a child's own parents is how the left is fulfilling its goal that "it takes a village (i.e., the government) to raise a child."

Third, unilateral divorce takes away fathers' rights because husbands have no defense against wives who want to dissolve the marriage just because they're tired of being married. Fourth, the meaning of marriage has been lost, which the high divorce rate demonstrates. Finally, the allegiance of family courts is no longer with protecting the sanctity of marriage but is with the institution of divorce. The primary concern is to make divorce fast and painless—and move it off the docket.

What we're left with, then, is the question: Are the consequences of unilateral divorce worth it?

To feminists, the answer is yes. Their support of unilateral divorce is not merely to achieve liberation from allegedly abusive marriages; it also is essential to the feminist goals of independence and empowerment of women. It serves their ultimate purpose of moving all wives, whether divorced or still married, into the labor force.

Before unilateral divorce, all fifty states made it the husband's obligation to support his wife and children. Unilateral divorce taught women the lesson that they could not depend on this support any longer. They must get a job and support themselves. And this new obligation on women spread rapidly, not only among those who were divorced but also among those who were happily married and worried about their future. That's why feminists such as Leslie Bennetts, author of *The Feminist Mistake*, try to scare women out of staying home with their children. Her argument is that when a wife opts out of the workforce, she sets herself up to be abandoned by a philandering husband.

At first unilateral divorce appeared to be a gift to men who sought to reclaim their youth by trading in a longtime, faithful wife and getting a trophy wife—one who's younger, thinner, and better looking. Husbands didn't always have to cough up much alimony because feminists had spread the notion that since homemakers are "parasites," alimony is demeaning. Women, they said, should be independent and support themselves.

But then feminists used their political clout to create a giant federal child-support enforcement bureaucracy, which favors mother-custody of the children and treats the father as good only for a paycheck. Divorce usually turns the man into a weakened, weekend father who is only a visitor in his child's life. Stephen Baskerville, author of *Taken into Custody*, explains:

> Like custody, (child support) is awarded ostensibly without reference to "fault," and yet disobedience brings swift and severe punishments. . . . Child support today has nothing to do with fathers abandoning their children, reneging on their marital vows, or even agreeing to a divorce. It is automatically assessed on all non-custodial parents, even those divorced over their objections and who lose their children through no legal fault or agreement of their own. . . . Like custody, in other words, child support has nothing to do with justice. On the other hand, it is a punitive measure, enforced with police, courts, and incarceration.[24]

At the time Ronald Reagan signed the California no-fault divorce into law, Americans accepted the idea as reasonable. But after seeing the fallout, many have changed their minds. Ronald Reagan's son Michael wrote in his book *Twice Adopted*, "Dad later said that he regretted signing the no-fault divorce bill and that he believed it was one of the worst mistakes he ever made in office. That law set in motion one of the most damaging social experiments in the history of our nation."[25]

THE WAR ON FATHERS

Here's what we know. Most social problems come from homes where children grow up without their own fathers. These problems include (but are not limited to) drug abuse, promiscuity, unwanted pregnancies, school dropouts, runaways, suicides, and crime. An estimated twenty-one million children in the United States today live in homes without their biological fathers. While there are some bad fathers in the world, no evidence exists that nearly half of American children have been voluntarily abandoned by their own fathers; feminists drove them out.

Back in the 1970s, feminists argued that parenting duties should be split evenly between wives and husbands. *Ms.* magazine floated premarital contracts that spelled out fathers' diaper-changing and other baby-care duties, and the National Organization for Women passed resolutions stating, "The father has equal responsibility with the mother for the child care role."

But after unilateral divorce was adopted and divorces became easy to get, feminists did an about-face. They demanded complete legal and physical custody and control of their children. Suddenly, the ex-husband became targeted as an essential breadwinner and the ex-wife became eager to proclaim her financial dependence on him. Many divorced feminists want the father out of sight, except for a few hours a month of visitation—at her discretion.

One explanation for the change is that the more time a

mother gets as custodial parent, the more money she can get the court to order to be paid by the father. And there is no accounting for how she spends the money, or even whether or not she allows her ex-husband the visitation hours he was awarded. Indeed, family courts are biased toward women because they are filled with politically correct judges who have been just as influenced by feminist dogma as everyone else.

A 1979 book by Lenore Walker called *The Battered Woman* is credited with originating what is known as the "Battered Woman Syndrome." Clearly there are battered women in America, but this book is primarily hearsay and overstates the problem. Walker admitted that her "research" and generalizations were based on "a self-volunteered sample" of women who contacted her after hearing her speeches or interviews. Although she mentions the domestic violence study undertaken by the National Institute of Mental Health, she fails to tell readers that its final conclusion was that women initiate violence in intimate relationships *at least as often* as men do!

Despite its lack of credibility, Walker's book spread the propaganda that the "battered" are always women and that "batterers" are always men. It argues that "battering" is not necessarily a violent, or even a physical act—one can be battered verbally as well. While it is true psychological abuse is real and very damaging, it is, unfortunately, subjective. Moreover, it's unfair to pretend that verbal abuse is perpetrated only by men against women and not vice versa. Women are just as capable of being nasty with words.

Our point is not that domestic violence isn't real, or that the physical abuse women suffer at the hands of men isn't worse than it is for men who suffer physical abuse—men are stronger than women and obviously can cause more harm. Assault and battery are crimes in every state, and when they occur, the victim should be protected and the perpetrator promptly punished. But we cannot overlook the facts that women are capable of being physically abusive, too, and that both sexes are equally capable of being emotionally and verbally abusive.

The problem we face in America is that domestic violence has become whatever women want to allege, with or without evidence. The domestic violence checklist typically provided by family courts to women seeking divorce and/or sole child custody asks them "if the other parent has *ever* done or threatened to do any of the following": "blaming all problems on you," "following you," "embarrassing, putting you down," "interrupting your eating or sleeping." Such actions are not illegal or criminal. People do not have a right not to be insulted. But today, acts that are not criminal between strangers have been made crimes between members of a household, and such actions can be punished by depriving fathers of their parental rights.

The Violence Against Women Act (VAWA) is a central element of feminist tactics. Passed in 1994, VAWA was President Bill Clinton's payoff to feminists who supported his nomination and election in 1992. Known as feminist pork, this law has been streaming, without accountability, nearly a billion dollars a year into the hands of feminists who use it to preach their anti-marriage and anti-male ideology, promote divorce, bias the family court system against men, lobby for feminist state laws, and engage in political advocacy.

Only five states define domestic violence in terms of overt physical actions that can be objectively proven or refuted in a court of law. The others use a definition that blurs the difference between violent action and run-of-the-mill marital arguments. An American Bar Association report states: "Domestic violence does not necessarily involve physical violence."

VAWA also finances the reeducation of judges and law enforcement personnel to teach them feminist stereotypes about male abusers and female victims, how to game the system to

empower women, and how to ride roughshod over the constitutional rights of men. Husbands and fathers are forced to endure
psychological reeducation in feminist ideology. Accused men
are assigned to classes where feminists teach shame and guilt
because of the alleged vast male conspiracy to subjugate women.

A Santa Fe, New Mexico, family court judge granted a
temporary restraining order against TV talk show host David
Letterman to protect a woman he had never met, never heard
of, and who lived two thousand miles away. Colleen Nestler
claimed Letterman had caused her "mental cruelty" and "sleep
deprivation" by using code words and gestures during his net-
work television broadcasts. Nestler met the definition of New
Mexico's statute against domestic violence because she claimed
she suffered "severe emotional distress." She claimed she saw
coded messages on Letterman's TV program for eleven years,
and that meant they had a "continuing relationship" and
(under the statute) that made him a "household member."
The restraining order was later dismissed, but the case was not
a judicial anomaly; it was the logical culmination of years of
ever-expanding definitions of domestic violence.

Family court judges issue two million restraining orders every
year—85 percent against men. Half do not include any evidence of violence but rely on vague complaints made without
proof or even evidence. Too often, a restraining order is just an
easy way for one spouse to get revenge or the upper hand in a
divorce or child custody dispute. The *Illinois Bar Journal* (June
2005) explained that restraining orders can "become part of the
gamesmanship of divorce." Once an order is issued, it becomes
nearly impossible for a father to retain or regain custody or even
get to see his own children. "Right under our noses, massive
systemic injustice is being visited upon fathers, threatening the
very fundamentals of family, society, and democracy," wrote
Todd M. Aglialoro in a review of Stephen Baskerville's book,

Taken Into Custody: The War against Fatherhood, Marriage, and the Family.[26]

Why, we might ask, don't Americans know about these injustices that are visited on men? For the same reason people don't know about any news that paints women in an unfavorable light—feminist bias. "To the media elites, the idea that men in divorce and custody cases might be part of an oppressed class is an alien concept," wrote Bernard Goldberg in *Bias*.[27]

WHAT DO WE TELL OUR SONS?

What do we tell our sons about the unfair world feminists have created? How will we help them navigate the hostile terrain?

We can start by raising them to be courageous, principled, and capable of thinking for themselves. Encourage them to embrace their masculinity. When little boys pick up a hairbrush and pretend it's a gun, let them. When they can't sit still in school, don't medicate them. When they like throwing a football around with their dads, do everything in your power to stay happily married to their dads so your boys can do this. When they want to play sports, find a college where Title IX has not wiped out their favorite sports. Teach your sons the virtue of "manliness," which Harvard professor Harvey Mansfield defines (in his book of the same name) as "confidence in the face of risk." Men's role as protector remains vital to civilization.

Most important, educate your sons about feminism. Tell them how it has harmed society. Tell them to look for a woman who's conservative in nature and hasn't fallen into the feminist trap. Let them know that no matter what the culture says, a husband's contribution to his family is every bit as important as the wife's. Tell them not to follow a girlfriend's career path, but to find a woman who is willing to follow his career path if they plan to have children. Because if he marries her, chances are she's going to land right back in the spot where women have always wanted to be: at home with their babies. As Carolyn Graglia has written:

> For [the anti-feminist woman], marriage is not a relationship of independent individuals who share living quarters while working towards separate, equally important lifetime career goals. Rather, it is a complementary relationship binding man and woman into a single marital unit: he provides the financial support while she assumes responsibility for the care and well-being of children which make the unit thrive. His career must be more important than her own. Only his employment can free her from the workplace to rear their children at home.[28]

These things require planning and maturity on the part of young men. Unfortunately, most young men today have been raised by baby boomers who have been seduced by feminist dogma and lack maturity themselves. As Reb Bradley points out in his excellent book, *Born Liberal, Raised Right*, "American parents, conservatives included, are increasingly raising liberal children."[29]

Bradley's explanation for why the modern generation has succumbed to politically correct ideology is that baby boomer parents have failed to raise their children with self-control, wisdom, and responsibility. Children have been raised by "indulgent protectors" (aka liberals) who see themselves as good, caring agents of change. Rather than focusing on time-tested values, such as duty, honor, sacrifice, and responsibility, boomers taught their children liberal values, such as tolerance, victimhood, and self-gratification. He concedes it is difficult for Americans to hear that their parents have dropped the ball, but if we want to solve the problems we face today, "the next generation of parents must change how they rear their children."[30]

Most important, we must begin by telling our sons (and daughters) the truth about what feminism has done. After all, no society can thrive—or survive—when half its members believe they're oppressed and the other half are told there's no reason for them to exist.

· 8 ·

A NEW ROAD MAP FOR WOMEN

It is in society's best interest to dismantle feminism.
Contented women will do less harm—and probably more
good—to society than frenzied and despairing ones.

—Carolyn Graglia

Social trends are extremely powerful. Once they become
ingrained in society, as feminism has, a sort of psychology
unfolds. Psychology is described in textbooks as "the science of
behavior"—a way of understanding why we react to our environment the way we do. "If [we] generally adhere to the laws of
the culture in which [we] live," wrote psychotherapist Dr. Raymond Lloyd Richmond, "and *if you are satisfied with [your] life*,
then there is no problem."[1] However, he says, many things in
our culture are socially acceptable but nevertheless pose a threat
to our emotional and spiritual lives. When people succumb to
them, life lets us know it. First, we get a gentle nudge; then,
he wrote, we get a "kick in the butt" through the repetition of
unpleasant conflicts. And if there is still no response, the rug
can be pulled out from under us.

The rug has been pulled out from under American women.
All signs point to it: the casual sex epidemic; the unrelenting
focus on women's victimhood and working mothers' guilt; our

doubts about the need for marriage; the belief that divorce is the answer to what ails us; and the recent study by the National Bureau of Economic Research that shows women's happiness has measurably declined since 1970. "Social change doesn't happen overnight: It takes decades for momentum to build and for the once-radical edge to become mainstream," wrote Dr. Jean M. Twenge.[2]

Since 1970, Americans have become accustomed to thinking about "a woman's place" in negative terms. As feminism slowly seeped into the fabric of our culture, Americans of all stripes began adapting to its cause. In so doing, we've dismissed the fact that there's an entirely different perspective from which to view the role of women in society.

The concept of women's rights is often thought of in the same context as civil rights. Feminists claim that what they call the "women's movement" is just like the civil rights movement—they pretend women were slaves to men in the same way blacks were slaves to whites. So they demand that all our laws be made gender-neutral as they have been made race-neutral. This is an unfair and absurd parallel. Nevertheless, feminists use it to get people to believe that what they are after is a good thing.

What women on the left really want, of course, has nothing to do with equality for women. Their goal is the same as President Obama's: to "fundamentally transform" America. Like Obama, feminists don't like America the way it is and want to change it. That's what they've wanted since the day they took to the streets in the 1960s.

Equality for women had nothing to do with it.

Americans have been hoodwinked. Today's men and women are not living in harmony, nor are they living up to their respective potential now that women in America have supposedly been liberated. Rather, there is an enormous chasm between men and women, and a bona fide culture war regarding gender roles.

Many people don't know what they think anymore because feminism has changed the culture and the language so drastically.

Does rejecting feminism mean rejecting women's equality? No, because that's not what feminism is about. Rejecting feminism means recognizing that women don't need feminism to make them equal to men because they already *are* equal—just not the same. Does rejecting feminism mean rejecting women's liberation? Yes—*if* liberation means liberating women from marriage and motherhood. We have learned the hard way that there is nothing empowering about ignoring one's biology.

When Sarah Palin entered the national spotlight in 2008, she compelled Americans to revisit feminism. For the first time since the revolution began, Americans have begun publicly debating feminism's modern relevance and long-term effects. We wonder whether feminism matters anymore; we wonder where feminism is headed; and we wonder what feminism means for the modern conservative movement. Many wonder whether Sarah Palin represents a "new" feminism or the death of feminism.

This conversation is unnecessary.

It doesn't matter whether people identify as 1970s (i.e., liberal or leftist) feminists, conservative feminists, or even non-feminists—most Americans think like a feminist even as they vociferously deny being one. They believe men and women should be considered equal not in *worth*, for that's a given, but in biology, physiology, and psychology. They believe men and women should approach life in the same way when it comes to sex, marriage, careers, and children. They believe that if it weren't for feminists, women would be considered inferior to men.

But that is all false propaganda, so there's no reason for conservatives to align themselves with feminism. In *Letters to a Young Conservative*, Dinesh D'Souza wrote, "I am a conservative because I believe conservatives have an accurate

THE FLIPSIDE OF FEMINISM

understanding of human nature and liberals do not."[3] That is the same number-one fatal flaw of feminists. These women, and the men in their lives, do not have an accurate view of human nature. By denying the differences between males and females, they set themselves up for failure. That's why feminists are such an angry and disagreeable bunch. It's impossible *not* to be bitter when you're banging your head against the wall, trying to keep the sun from rising.

If you ask any woman today who has young children and a full-time job, or any woman who sleeps around indiscriminately, or even the average middle-class single mom who most likely initiated her divorce, she's likely to say she's not a feminist. (All public opinion surveys report that the majority of women do not want to be called feminists.) Indeed, she has probably never joined a feminist cause in her life, nor does she necessarily have a strong opinion on the matter. *But her lifestyle is a direct result of feminism's influence in her life.* That is the insidious nature of the feminist revolution, and it is the reason why it's the most significant social movement of our time. Undoing the damage will not be easy—but it is possible.

ADMITTING THE PROBLEM IS HALF THE BATTLE

They say alcoholics can't change until they admit they have a problem—this same approach can be applied to any conflict. Recognizing that feminism failed in its mission, that it is based on faulty assumptions and arguments, and that it drives a wedge between men and women and even among women, is the first step to recovery.

For those who fell into the feminist trap, this may mean having to make some serious changes—either with one's lifestyle or one's attitude. This can be daunting, but people make life changes all the time. Some folks change careers; some folks change lifestyles; some folks even change religions. Change can happen—but admitting the problem is half the battle.

Feminist journalist and author Anne Taylor Fleming issues a warning. Thirty years ago, Fleming argued that if she got pregnant unexpectedly, she'd have an abortion—she was adamantly opposed to pro-life arguments. Twenty years later, in her book *Motherhood Deferred*, Fleming wrote, "I am a woman of forty who put career ahead of motherhood and now longs for motherhood. . . . I belong to the sisterhood of the infertile. I am a lonesome, babyless baby boomer now completely consumed by the longing for a baby. . . . I am tempted to roll down the window and shout 'Hey, hey, Gloria, Germaine, Kate. Tell us, how does it feel to have ended up without babies, children, flesh of your flesh. Was your ideology worth the empty womb?'"[4]

Germaine Greer, the 1970s feminist icon who encouraged women to reject motherhood, also paid the ultimate price. "I was desperate for a baby and I have the medical bills to prove it. I still have pregnancy dreams, waiting for something that will never happen."[5]

But it is Rebecca Walker, daughter of committed feminist Alice Walker, who wrote *The Color Purple* (which was revered by the feminist elite and made into a major motion picture and Broadway musical) who was the most courageous in telling the truth about feminism in an article entitled, "How My Mother's Fanatical Views Tore Us Apart":

As a child, I . . . yearned for a traditional mother. . . . I grew up believing that children are millstones around your neck, and the idea that motherhood can make you happy is a complete fairytale. . . . When I hit my 20s, . . . I could feel my biological clock ticking, but I felt if I listened to it, I would be betraying my mother and all she had taught me. . . . In fact, having a child has been the most rewarding experience of my life. . . . My only regret is that I discovered the joys of motherhood so late—I have been trying for a second child, but so far with no luck.

Feminism has betrayed an entire generation of women into childlessness. . . . But far from taking responsibility for this, the leaders of the women's movement close ranks against anyone who dares to question them—as I have learned to my cost. . . . I believe feminism is an experiment, and all experiments need to be assessed on their results. Then, when you see huge mistakes have been paid, you need to make alterations.[6]

The cultural shift in American women's plans for the future—toward big careers, rather than motherhood—has resulted in many unfulfilled dreams. The childless women above who regret their choices may represent the extreme result of feminism, but millions of modern women needlessly face fertility battles simply because no one told them not to focus so obsessively on careers, or to find careers that work well with motherhood. No one told them that getting academic degree after degree may be counterproductive if having children is part of their life plan.

The result is that young women give babies no thought whatsoever until they're holding their own in their arms. Only then do their previous plans fall away, and women find themselves in a quandary. Because they didn't *assume* they'd be out of the workforce caring for babies, women are left with an unbearable choice: they either put their children in day care, or they rethink their entire life plan.

A modern woman who wants to determine whether she's living an authentic life should ask herself if the choices she has made reflect *her* values, or whether she's simply doing what everyone around her is doing. Have you engaged in casual sex because it's "the thing to do" and felt regret afterward? Do you want to get married but don't dare admit it? Is the pursuit of a career alongside motherhood something you think you need in order to feel complete? Are your husband and children unhappy because you are consumed by your career? Have you rejected marriage and are regretting it? If you answered yes to any of these questions, *that's* feminism, whether you recognize it as such or not. The life you're living was supposed to make you feel fulfilled. Has it?

American women don't have to succumb to bitterness and discontent. The first step to taking back control—to being truly empowered—is to reject feminism. This isn't a matter of being rigid (though people may tell you otherwise); it's a matter of accepting the truth. It is simply impossible to defend feminism once you know the facts.

The challenge will be to remove yourself from the culture and determine what *you* really want. Most women (most *people*) are conservative in nature. Conservatism is a natural state because it accepts human nature as it is, rather than trying to fight it. Conservative women believe in a universal moral order that makes demands on them. Those who acknowledge that there are differences between men and women and who strive to meet moral standards (even though they may fail from time to time) are far more content than those who do not.

Women in America *can* have everything they want out of life, but they must first break free from feminist assumptions and distortions. For some, this means ignoring their own mothers; for others, their professors or bosses. For all of us, it means rejecting the confused, unhappy, dissatisfied spin sisters in the media. They have not figured out what life is about, nor will they ever figure it out—their belief that women are victims clouds their vision.

We must stop talking about women's rights, women's needs, women's problems, and progress for women. We must stop talking about girl power and female empowerment, and about overturning a patriarchy that doesn't exist. When we frame the debate in feminist lingo, we foster a war between the sexes. It's time to end the war between the sexes. Men are not the enemy.

THE PEDESTAL

Now that we know what we need to do, *how* do we do it? We start by bringing back mutual respect. Men and women used to have respect for one another before feminism came along. They knew gender differences were real, so there was no need to fight over The Pedestal—each gender had its own pedestal. Wives respected their husbands as breadwinners, and husbands were in awe of their wives' maternal capabilities. That didn't mean men didn't help with domestic duties or women never worked outside the home (contrary to what feminists told us). But men tended to defer to women on matters related to the home, and women tended to defer to men when it came to making family income decisions.

Research proves this is still the case. On September 25, 2008, Pew Research Center reported that in 43 percent of American couples, the wives make more decisions about household finances, weekend activities, and home purchases. Husbands make these decisions for only 25 percent of couples, while 31 percent split decision making between husband and wife. Even if a husband makes more money, the wife is still more likely to decide how the money is spent.

Unfortunately, once feminism came along, women abandoned their pedestal in droves and decided they wanted to share the man's pedestal with him. They claimed they wanted both sexes on the same pedestal to represent equality and prove men and women are the same. Instead they found themselves in conflict. Since there isn't enough room on a pedestal for both of them, feminists pushed men off to make room for themselves. Remember Maria Shriver's statement? "As we move into this phase we're calling a woman's nation, women can turn their pivotal role as wage-earners, as consumers, as bosses, as opinion-shapers, as co-equal partners in whatever we do into a potent force for change. Emergent economic power gives women a new seat at the table—at the head of the table."[7]

That's not equality. That's a matriarchy.

The only way to restore mutual respect between the sexes is for women to get off the man's pedestal and climb back up on their own. When each sex has his or her own pedestal, their unique biology is respected, and conflict naturally diminishes. By trying to share the same pedestal, men and women deny each other's inherent natures. That's why there are many women today who, when they decide they actually want to stay home with their children, face resistance from their own husbands who don't want to give up the income from their wives' jobs!

Sex is a problem, too. More and more wives today say they're too tired for sex. In a nationwide Women's Wellness Survey published in *Cooking Light* magazine, "having enough sex" was number *seven* on women's list of priorities—after "getting enough sleep," "keeping stress level low," "finding time to relax," "eating healthfully," "drinking the recommended amount of water," and "finding time to exercise." Naturally, this poses a problem for husbands, who are rarely too tired for sex. Sex is a man's favorite pastime, and the wives who are too tired to have it are often resentful of this fact.

If change is going to come, it will have to come from

women—they are the ones who changed the natural order of things. Moreover, men aren't the ones who kvetch about their place in the world—not because they have it so great (contrary to feminist dogma), but because it's not in their nature. Men tend to go along with whatever women say they need.

That's why men's attitudes about "a woman's place" have changed right along with women's! Just about the only thing that hasn't changed for men is their sexual nature—*that* they can't do anything about. Having sex with their wives is one way husbands demonstrate their love, and when wives turn away from them on a routine basis, as women admit they are now doing, that's perceived as rejection. Turning away from one's husband in bed is akin to a wife walking up to her husband to put her arms around him, but he turns his back and walks away. (Both of these scenarios are the reason many extramarital affairs begin.)

THE NON-NEGOTIABLES

Rejecting feminism and restoring mutual respect for both sexes are prerequisites for moving forward. But there's another crucial element: the non-negotiables. There are many things in life that people consider non-negotiable. If we choose to go on a diet, there are probably foods we know we aren't able or willing to give up, and we're likely to choose a plan that allows us to eat those foods. This same theory applies when mapping out our lives: some things for women should be non-negotiable. Here are three reasonable assumptions smart women make:

1. Casual sex is a dead-end street, and cohabitation does not lead to a successful marriage.

2. Marriage is the ultimate goal, and divorce should not be assumed to be an option.

3. Children need, deserve, and want to be raised by their own parents, who are married to each other.

Recognizing that "sleeping around" leads only to disappointment, women stand a better chance of avoiding STDs and heartache. Similarly, if women view marriage as a positive thing, and assume divorce is not an option, their chance of choosing the right spouse increases. (Obviously, divorce is always an option. But *assuming* marriage is a lifelong contract is the key.) "Those who see marriage as a nonreversible commitment will be more inclined to do the psychological work that makes them feel satisfied with their decision than will those whose attitude about marriage is more relaxed," wrote Barry Schwartz in *The Paradox of Choice*.[8]

Finally, women should assume they will *want* to stay home with their children, at least during the early years. This increases the likelihood that they'll do the necessary planning that will allow this to happen.

When women embrace these three non-negotiables, the possibilities of happiness become greater—and women avoid feeling stuck later on, as though they've been victimized. "It is time to leave the question of the role of women up to Mother Nature—a difficult lady to fool. You have only to give women the same opportunities as men, and you will soon find out what is or is not in their nature. What is in women's nature to do they will do, and you won't be able to stop them. But you will also find, and so will they, that what is not in their nature, even if they are given every opportunity, they will not do—and you won't be able to make them do it," wrote Clare Boothe Luce.[9]

GOING FORWARD

When someone calls our basic beliefs into question, it takes time to mull it over. Americans aren't used to hearing that women are the fortunate sex, or that "hooking up" is wrong (and foolish), or that happy lifetime marriages are attainable, or that staying home to care for one's children is a noble and worthwhile endeavor, or that men in America are the real second-class citizens.

But it *is* possible to shift the paradigm.

Those who believe women in America have not yet achieved equality or that American women are somehow oppressed and need government intervention to level the playing field, think they're fighting a nation that has wronged them. In reality, they are fighting human nature.

We know it's difficult to ignore the culture and do your own thing. While many people do, they are not the norm. "Most people, especially young people, need to be confirmed by the community in which they live. They cannot beyond a certain limit establish for themselves a system of their own verities and preferences," wrote Midge Decter in *An Old Wife's Tale.*[10]

The "verities and preferences" American women have been exposed to for the past several decades have been mostly of a left-wing nature. Those who mentored today's generation are baby boomers, and they became modern women's role models. Many are committed feminists, and others went along with feminist ideology even if they had reservations about it or didn't realize they were going along with it. Baby boomers supplanted the Greatest Generation's good advice with advice that belies wisdom and common sense.

Of course we can't blame everything on feminists. There has been a dramatic change in the culture itself. In previous generations, the preferences of most Americans were generally confirmed by their communities. Technology didn't play a big role in people's lives, so their worlds were smaller. Close-knit communities and family ties, along with the universal moral order that was once in place, meant Americans were mostly exposed to people who lived like they did—conservatively.

Today, this world is gone. Families are spread out; people rarely mill about in their neighborhoods but are instead glued to their television sets and computers; and religious life is at an all-time low. Because of this, young people's preferences are now largely influenced by technology and mainstream media, all of which are very liberal.

This is not to suggest people can't think for themselves and merely copy what they see. But it does mean that when people are routinely bombarded with a certain ideology—whether it's conservative, liberal, or some variation thereof—they are going to be affected by it. Most people crave acceptance.

Those who want to live a more conservative or traditional lifestyle will need to seek validation elsewhere. To a large degree, they will have to remove themselves from pop culture and find others who share their beliefs and lifestyle. (Author Marybeth Hicks explains how parents can do this in her excellent book, *Bringing Up Geeks*.) It is unfortunate, to be sure, that Americans have to go to such lengths to stay true to their principles—it's much easier to have the culture agree with you. But that is where we are. Every time we open a newspaper or magazine, every time we turn on the television set or even our computers, we are barraged with messages that run counter to the values Americans once held dear.

Take, for example, some of the movies that were released in 2010—the ones we mentioned earlier. In one summer alone, four major motion pictures—*Eat, Pray, Love*, *The Switch*, *The Kids Are All Right*, and *The Back-Up Plan*—laud the ultra-liberal notion that children don't need fathers, and marriage is oppressive to women.

In the February 2010 issue of *O* magazine, the editors list "100 things that have improved in America." Here is a sampling of the "improvements": gay marriage has been legalized in Iowa; the "boys' club" has been cracked by actress Kathryn Bigelow; single motherhood has "never been friendlier," in part because "battery-operated companionship" (aka vibrators) has replaced the need for sexual intercourse; and the "aloof breadwinners [dads] of yesteryear have been replaced by full participants in the diapering, the disciplining, and the loving"—implying that traditional fathers were not loving and did not discipline their children, both of which are patently false and insulting to older men.

These movies and articles do not help Americans move forward in a positive direction. Indeed, they would have been unthinkable a couple of decades ago. Such messages could only occur in a country that equates feminism with "progress." In the 1960s, these scenarios were considered radical notions. Forty years later, they are mainstream.

Fortunately, smart women—aka conservatives and independents—know they are still radical notions, and not something to which any society should adhere. That's why we've seen a resurgence of conservatism in America—people know in their gut when something is off kilter. "What conservatism does is ask the question avoided by progressive promises: at what expense? [Progressives'] heedless pursuit of transformation reinvigorated a moribund conservative spirit," wrote Peter Berkowitz in the *Wall Street Journal*.[11]

Perhaps this spirit will translate to a new day in America when women don't need to define themselves using feminism as a benchmark. Hopefully, some day, women's magazines will glorify marriage and motherhood—rather than casual sex, divorce, "working mothers," and single motherhood. Is this possible? It will be a challenge. It may even require a social revolution.

Fortunately, one seems to be underway. In 2010, leading sociologist Geoff Dench analyzed responses to questions asked in the annual British Social Attitudes survey. The results were clear: *what women want is a husband who will be the main bread-winner.* In 1998, the number of British mothers who believe family life suffers when mothers work full-time was a mere 21 percent. By 2006, it increased to 37 percent. A similar spike occurred when women were asked whether they agreed that men and women should have different roles. In 2002, a mere 2 percent of mothers said yes. Four years later, it jumped to *17 percent,* an enormous leap in a very short period of time.

The reason for the turnaround, according to Dench, is that there has been a gradual move toward more respect for the work mothers do at home, and while the number of mothers in the workforce has increased, the number reflects mainly part-time work. The women who appear happiest, he says, are those who value motherhood and homemaking—who embrace the traditional female role along with *some form* of paid work.

American attitudes are similar. Not only has the number of women who have opted out of the workforce to stay home with their children grown in recent years, the overwhelming majority of married women prefer part-time rather than full-time employment. Most mothers stay home with their children when they're young and often return to the workforce when their children are in school.

If there is indeed a social revolution under way, it shouldn't stop with women's choice to honor their nature. It must also include a newfound respect for men. It was New York City's fire*men* who dared to charge up the stairs of the burning Twin

Towers on September 11, 2001. The death tally of New York City's firefighters was: men 343, women 0. Can anyone honestly say you would have wanted a woman coming to your rescue on that fateful day?

Men's physical prowess isn't the only reason they deserve respect. The feminist elite love to harp on the idea that men don't understand women—"[Men] don't understand what women feel," says Oprah. But women don't understand what men feel either. Women cannot understand the feelings of the man who has the well-being of his family *absolutely depend* on his job. Every day husbands get up, take a shower, and go to work for eight to ten (or twelve?) hours so their wives can be liberated from the demands of a full-time job. It is men's *consistent* work that provides women the freedom and flexibility to do as they please with their lives.

Indeed, men live in their own kind of prison—they usually don't up and leave their jobs or their wives in order to "find themselves." Many forfeit the kinds of lives they, too, might prefer because they know it wouldn't be good for their families. That's called sacrifice, a concept women on the left routinely eschew. Men also don't have an excuse to leave their jobs if they're unhappy. Women do. If women want to leave the workforce, motherhood is a perfectly sound reason to do so—and a good society encourages this. As former working mother Sarah Amsbary learned the hard way, "Maternity provides an escape hatch that paternity does not. Having a baby provides a graceful and convenient exit."[12]

With the advances in technology and Americans' increased longevity, there has never been a better time for women to have it all. A feminist or left-wing approach to life will not help women achieve this goal. A conservative approach will. "Society has been weakened by its curtailing of women's domestic role, which contributes substantially—possibly more than any other single activity—to societal health and stability. All indicia of familial well-being demonstrate that our society was a significantly better place for families in the decade before the feminist revival," wrote Graglia.[13]

Being conservative isn't just about one's politics—there are many conservative Democrats in America—conservatism is a lifestyle. Not all conservative women are alike in their style, demeanor, or behavior; but they do share several key traits: they are cautious, practical, and smart. That doesn't mean conservative women don't make mistakes. But it does mean they stand a better chance at getting it right.

Philosophers have long since concluded that everyone has the potential to live a happy life. Even Abraham Lincoln said most folks are only as happy as they make up their minds to be.

For women, the answer lies in our decision to be satisfied.

THE TEN FEMINIST COMMANDMENTS

1. Thou shalt have lots of sex with lots of different men.

2. Thou shalt be allowed to have an abortion at any time for any reason.

3. Thou shalt ignore thy biological clock and, if necessary, create new methods of conception.

4. Thou shalt pursue demanding careers and pay other women to raise thy children.

5. Thou shalt not feel guilty about pursuing demanding careers and paying other women to raise thy children.

6. Thou shalt be allowed to divorce at any time and keep custody of the children.

7. Thou shalt be artificially inseminated if thou doesn't get married but still wants children.

8. Thou shalt belittle men until their manhood is gone.

9. Thou shalt not take thine husband's name.

10. Thou shalt demean all full-time homemakers and conservative women.

APPENDIX B

SENSE & SEXUALITY:

EXCERPTS FROM
THE COLLEGE GIRL'S GUIDE TO REAL
PROTECTION IN A HOOKED-UP WORLD

by Miriam Grossman, M.D.

Copyright © 2008 Clare Boothe Luce Policy Institute

HOOKING UP

A recent study of the hook-up culture at Princeton University reveals that before the hook-up, girls expect emotional involvement almost twice as often as guys, and 34 percent hope "a relationship might evolve." Guys, more than girls, are in part motivated by hopes of improving their social reputation, or of bragging about their exploits to friends the next day.

After the hook-up, 91 percent of girls admit to having feelings of regret, at least occasionally. Guilt and "feeling used" are commonly cited, and overall, 80 percent of girls wish the hook-up hadn't happened. Other studies have shown that 84 percent of women said that after having sex a few times, even with someone they didn't want to be emotionally involved with, they begin to feel vulnerable and would at least like to know if the other person cares about them.

The Cervix

A woman's cervix has a vulnerable area one cell thick called the transformation zone. It's easy for HPV (the human papilloma virus, which can cause genital warts, and even cervical cancer) to settle in there. That's why most teen girls are infected from one of their first sexual partners. By adulthood the transformation zone is replaced with a thicker, tougher surface. So it's wise to delay sexual activity, or, if you've already started, to stop.

Even though these infections are common, and usually disappear with time, learning you have one can be devastating. Natural reactions are shock, anger, and confusion. *Who did I get this from, and when? Was he unfaithful? Who should I tell?* And hardest of all: *Who will want me now?* These concerns can affect your mood, concentration, and sleep. They can deal a serious blow to your self-esteem. And to your GPA.

The HPV vaccine is a major achievement, but the protection it provides is limited. You are still vulnerable to other infections like herpes, chlamydia, HIV, and non-covered strains of HPV.

Risky Sex

Having more than five oral sex partners has been associated with throat cancer. Turns out that HPV can cause malignant tumors in the throat, just like it does in the cervix. In a study of sexually active college men, HPV was found both where you'd expect—the genital area—and where you wouldn't: under fingernails. Yes, you read that right. Researchers now speculate whether the virus can be shared during activities considered "safe," like mutual masturbation.

According to the Centers for Disease Control, approximately 30 percent of all women will have had anal intercourse by the age of twenty-four. Even with condoms, this behavior places them at increased risk of infection with HIV and other STDs. For example, the risk for HIV transmission during anal intercourse is at least twenty times higher than with vaginal intercourse.

The government website, www.fda.gov, provides no-nonsense advice about avoiding HIV: "Condoms provide some protection, but anal intercourse is simply too dangerous to practice." Translation: The rectum is an exit, not an entrance.

OXYTOCIN: THE "TRUST" HORMONE

Intimate behavior floods a woman's brain with a chemical called oxytocin that fuels attachment. Cuddling, kissing, and sexual contact releases this chemical and says to the brain: "I'm with someone special now. Time to switch love on and caution off." When oxytocin levels are high, you're more likely to overlook your partner's faults and to take risks you otherwise wouldn't.

You do not want your brain drenched in this hormone when making critical decisions, such as What do I think of him? How far do I want this to go? You'll want to make these decisions before you get too close. Like alcohol, oxytocin turns a red light green. It plays a major role in what's called "the biochemistry of attachment." Because of it, you could develop strong feelings for a guy who's not the least bit interested in you.

WOMEN'S FERTILITY

Seventy-five percent of college freshmen say raising a family is an "essential or very important goal." But 55 percent of younger high-achieving women are childless at thirty-five, and 89 percent think they'll be able to get pregnant into their forties.

This is patently false. It is easiest for a woman to conceive and deliver a healthy child in her twenties. Fertility declines slightly at thirty, and more dramatically at thirty-five. Waiting rooms of fertility clinics are packed with health-conscious women who work out and count calories—they're there because they're forty years old.

Motherhood doesn't always happen when the time is right. There's a window of opportunity, then the window closes. Some women feel an unexpected longing for a child just as the window is closing.

www.miriamgrossmanmd.com

APPENDIX C

1991 NOW RESOLUTIONS[1]

• THE EQUAL RIGHTS AMENDMENT •

Whereas, the passing of the Equal Rights Amendment (ERA) is a priority of the National Organization for Women (NOW); and

Whereas, consciousness raising (CR) has been the backbone of chapters and their development; and

Whereas, the women new to NOW do not have a history of CR; and

Whereas, the process of CR is never ending; and

Whereas, through the CR process, women connect to women, and with this connection, we have strength and are empowered;

Therefore, be it resolved that National NOW inform chapter, state and regional leadership of the availability of materials, books and publicity to encourage CR to take place.

• FUNDING OF ABORTION •

Whereas, accessible abortion is a basic, fundamental right of every woman: and

Whereas, the United States government uses tax dollars to subsidize medical services through Medicare and Medicaid funding; and

Whereas, tax dollars should be available to pay for safe legal abortions so that the fundamental right to choose whether to carry a pregnancy to term can be equally accessible to all women regardless of socioeconomic status;

Therefore, be it resolved that the National Organization for Women (NOW) draft model legislation regarding funding at all levels for abortion and reproductive services in the states;

Be it further resolved that the Young Feminists can begin the struggle to win back and retain Medicaid funded abortions by organizing non-violent mass demonstrations calling for the repeal of all limitations on Medicaid abortions and call for free safe, legal abortions without restrictions.

• PARENTAL INVOLVEMENT LAWS •

Whereas, young women's lives are directly threatened by growing support for state laws requiring parental interference for abortions; and

Whereas, many such women are under the voting age and therefore wield little electoral power regarding this issue; and

Whereas, National NOW has already implemented a strong and far-reaching agenda actively opposing parental interference legislation; and

Whereas, National NOW is now officially working with young feminists to take control over their lives and their bodies;

Therefore, be it resolved that the NOW National board and NOW's membership include parental consent/notification as an issue on its young feminist action agenda. . . .

• LESBIAN AND GAY RIGHTS ACTIONS •

Whereas, Lesbian rights is one of the four priority issues of the National Organization for Women (NOW); and

Whereas, NOW supports Lesbian and Gay rights in all aspects and is working to achieve full incorporation of Lesbians and Gays in all aspects of society; and

Whereas, it is essential for NOW to continue to be visible and active in our support of Lesbian and Gay rights;

Therefore, be it resolved that NOW supports the following national actions:

1. The Annual National Coming Out Day activities; and

2. The April, 1993 March on Washington for

3. Lesbian and Gay Rights. . . .

• WOMEN IN COMBAT •

Whereas, during the Equal Rights Amendment fight, our opposition effectively fanned the flames of fear that women would be drafted and thrown into foxholes in some strange and distant country; and

Whereas, with women soldiers playing a more significant role in the Persian Gulf than ever before in our military history, we may have an unprecedented opportunity to bring to an end the long debate over whether women should be in combat, to expand career opportunities for women in the military and to remove what has been an overwhelming obstacle to women's equality and the Equal Rights Amendment; and

Whereas, exclusion of women from positions arbitrarily defined as "combat" is based on archaic ideas of what women and men are physically and emotionally capable of doing and outdated ideas of what modern military theory and combat are; and . . .

Whereas, the exclusion of women from combat in the modern military is a fraud only to perpetuate a second class status of women in the military; economically and educationally disadvantaged young women cannot use the armed services, which are the largest vocational training grounds in the U.S., in the same way young men can to help themselves; young men can join, get training, a possibility of a pension and often veteran's preferences in hiring when they leave the military; young women face higher entrance requirements and quotas limiting the numbers of women who get into the military—and once they get in, women receive less training and fewer promotions; women are almost 11% of the military, but fill only .9% of the military's top 1000 officers' jobs and only about .8% of the top 15,000 senior enlisted positions; and

Whereas, the combat exclusion hurts our country's defense and foreign policy; women are effectively eliminated from most highranking leadership positions in the military by being excluded from career-enhancing, command positions defined as "combat"; and with women and women's perspective missing from the Joint Chiefs of Staff and other military policy bodies, our country's public policy is the poorer; . . .

Therefore, be it resolved, that NOW demands equality for women in joining the military and in training, job assignments and benefits in the military; and

Be it further resolved, that NOW actively supports elimination of statutory restrictions on women in the military.

BIBLIOGRAPHY

*MUST-READ BOOKS
(that you'll never hear about on Oprah)

*Basham, Megan. *Beside Every Successful Man: Getting the Life You Want by Helping Your Husband Get Ahead.* New York: Three Rivers Press, 2009.

*Baskerville, Steven. *Taken into Custody: The War against Fathers, Marriage, and the Family.* Nashville: Cumberland House, 2007.

*Bernard, Michelle. *Women's Progress: How Women Are Wealthier, Healthier, and More Independent Than Ever Before.* Dallas: Spence Publishing, 2007.

*Blyth, Myrna. *Spin Sisters: How the Women of the Media Sell Unhappiness and Liberalism to the Women of America.* New York: St. Martin's Press, 2004.

*Bradley, Reb. *Born Liberal, Raised Right: How to Rescue America from Moral Decline—One Family at a Time.* Los Angeles: WND Books, 2008.

Brennan, Bridget. *Why She Buys: The New Strategy for Reaching the World's Most Powerful Consumers.* New York: Crown Business, 2009.

*Brizendine, Louann. *The Male Brain: A Breakthrough Understanding of How Men and Boys Think.* New York: Broadway Books, 2010.

Bronson, Po and Ashley Merryman. *NurtureShock: New Thinking about Children.* New York: Twelve, 2009.

*Brooks, Arthur C. *Who Really Cares: The Surprising Truth about Compassionate Conservatism.* New York: Basic Books, 2006.

*Bruce, Tammy. *The New Thought Police: Inside the Left's Assault on Free Speech and Free Minds.* New York: Forum Publishing, 2001.

Chynoweth, W. Edward. *Masquerade: The Feminist Illusion.* Lanham, MD: Hamilton Books, 2005.

Cohen, Kerry. *Loose Girl: A Memoir of Promiscuity.* New York: Hyperion, 2008.

*Coulter, Ann. *Guilty: Liberal "Victims" and Their Assault on America.* New York: Three Rivers Press, 2009.

*Crenshaw, Dave. *The Myth of Multitasking: How Doing It All Gets Nothing Done.* New York: Jossey-Bass, 2008.

*Crittenden, Danielle. *What Our Mothers Didn't Tell Us: Why Happiness Eludes the Modern Woman.* New York: Simon & Schuster, 1999.

Dawson, Rosario and Andrea Wong. *Secrets of Powerful Women: Leading Change for a New Generation.* New York: Hyperion, 2010.

*Decter, Midge. *An Old Wife's Tale: My Seven Decades in Love and War.* New York: Regan Books, 2001.

*Dierker, Judge Robert H., Jr. *The Tyranny of Tolerance: A Sitting Judge Breaks the Code of Silence to Expose the Liberal Judicial Assault.* New York: Crown Forum, 2006.

*Doyle, R. F. *Save the Males: Masculinity and Men's Rights Redux.* Forest Lake, MN: Poor Richard's Press, revised 2010.

*Dreskin, William and Wendy. *The Day Care Decision.* New York: M. Evans and Co., 1983.

*D'Souza, Dinesh. *Letters to a Young Conservative.* New York: Basic Books, 2002.

*Eberstadt, Mary. *Home-Alone America: The Hidden Toll of Day Care, Behavioral Drugs, and Parent Substitutes.* New York: Sentinel, 2004.

*Farrell, Warren. *The Myth of Male Power.* New York: Simon & Schuster, 1993.

*———. *Why Men Earn More: The Startling Truth Behind the Pay Gap—and What Women Can Do about It.* New York: AMACOM, 2005.

Farber, David. *The Rise and Fall of Modern American Conservatism.* Princeton, NJ: Princeton University Press, 2010.

Friedan, Betty. *The Feminine Mystique.* New York: W. W. Norton & Co., 2001.

Gilbert, Elizabeth. *Eat, Pray, Love.* New York: Penguin, 2006.

———. *Committed: A Skeptic Makes Peace with Marriage.* New York: Viking, 2010.

*Gilder, George. *Men and Marriage.* Louisiana: Pelican Publishing, 1992.

*Goldberg, Bernard. *Bias: A CBS Insider Exposes Media Bias.* Washington D.C.: Regnery, 2001.

———. *100 People Who Are Screwing Up America.* New York: Harper Collins, 2005.

———. *Arrogance: Rescuing America from the Media Elite.* New York: Warner Books, 2003.

*Graglia, F. Carolyn. *Domestic Tranquility: A Brief against Feminism.* Dallas: Spence Publishing, 1998.

Greenberg, Cathy L., and Barrett S. Avigdor. *What Happy Working Mothers Know.* New York: Wiley, 2009.

*Grossman, Miriam. *You're Teaching My Child What? A Physician Exposes the Lies of Sex Education and How They Harm Your Child.* Washington D.C.: Regnery Publishing, 2010.

*Harper, Andre. *Political Emancipation: Observations from a Black Man Who Rejected Liberal Indoctrination.* California: Bookstand Publishing, 2009.

Kelley, Kitty. *Oprah: A Biography*. New York: Crown Publishers, 2010.

*Liebau, Carol Platt. *Prude: How the Sex-Obsessed Culture Damages Girls*. New York: Center Street Books, 2007.

*Lukas, Carrie. *The Politically Incorrect Guide to Women, Sex, and Feminism*. Washington D.C.: Regnery, 2006.

*Mansfield, Harvey C., *Manliness*. New Haven: Yale University Press, 2007.

*Marquardt, Elizabeth. *Between Two Worlds: The Inner Lives of Children of Divorce*. New York: Crown, 2005.

Mitchell, Brian. *Weak Link: The Feminization of the American Military*. Washington, D.C.: Regnery Gateway, 1989.

*O'Beirne, Kate. *Women Who Make the World Worse (and How Their Radical Feminist Assault Is Ruining Our Schools, Families, Military, and Sports)*. New York: Sentinel, 2006.

*O'Reilly, Bill. *The Culture Warrior*. New York: Broadway Books, 2007.

*Parker, Kathleen. *Save the Males: Why Men Matter[,] Why Women Should Care*. New York: Random House, 2008.

Paul, Pamela. *The Starter Marriage and the Future of Matrimony*. New York: Random House, 2002.

*Rhoads, Steven. *Taking Sex Differences Seriously*. New York: Encounter Books, 2004.

*Robertson, Brian C. *Day Care Deception: What the Child Care Establishment Isn't Telling Us.* New York: Encounter Books, 2003.

Saban, Cheryl. *What Is Your Self-Worth? A Woman's Guide to Validation.* New York: Hay House, 2009.

*Schlafly, Phyllis, ed. *Equal Pay for UNequal Work.* Washington D.C., Eagle Forum Education & Legal Defense Fund, 1983.

*Schlafly, Phyllis. *Feminist Fantasies.* Dallas: Spence Publishing, 2004.

*———. *The Power of the Positive Woman.* New York: Arlington House, 1977.

*———. ed. *Who Will Rock the Cradle?* Washington D.C.: Eagle Forum Education & Legal Defense Fund, 1989.

Schwartz, Barry. *The Paradox of Choice: Why More Is Less.* New York: Harper Collins, 2004.

*Shalit, Wendy. *A Return to Modesty: Discovering the Lost Virtue.* New York: Touchstone, 2000.

*———. *The Good Girl Revolution: Young Rebels with Self-Esteem and High Standards.* New York: Random House, 2008.

Stossel, John. *Myths, Lies, and Downright Stupidities: Why Everything You Know Is Wrong.* New York: Hyperion, 2006.

Twenge, Jean M. *Generation Me: Why Today's Young Americans Are More Confident, Assertive, Entitled—and More Miserable Than Ever Before.* New York: Free Press, 2007.

Twenge, Jean M., and W. Keith Campbell. *The Narcissism Epidemic: Living in the Age of Entitlement.* New York: Free Press, 2009.

*Venker, Suzanne. *7 Myths of Working Mothers: Why Children and (Most) Careers Just Don't Mix.* Dallas: Spence Publishing, 2004.

*Waite, Linda, and Maggie Gallagher. *The Case for Marriage: Why Married People Are Happier, Healthier, and Better Off Financially.* New York: Broadway Books, 2000.

*Wallerstein, Judith S., and Sandra Blakeslee. *The Good Marriage: How and Why Love Lasts.* New York: Warner Books, 1995.

*Wallerstein, Judith S., Julia Lewis, and Sandra Blakeslee. *The Unexpected Legacy of Divorce.* New York: Hyperion, 2000.

Weissbourd, Richard. *The Parents We Mean to Be: How Well-Intentioned Adults Undermine Children's Moral and Emotional Development.* New York: Houghton Mifflin, 2009.

Young-Eisendrath, Polly. *The Self-Esteem Trap: Raising Confident and Compassionate Kids in an Age of Self-Importance.* New York: Little, Brown, 2008.

NOTES

A NOTE FROM THE AUTHORS

1. Dana Loesch, "Sarah Palin and the rise of the Feminist Right," *Washington Examiner*, Columns and Opinions, August 22, 2010; emphasis added. http://www.washingtonexaminer.com/opinion/columns/Sarah-Palin-and-the-rise-of-the-Feminist-Right-534655-101265274.html

INTRODUCTION: CONSERVATIVE TRAILBLAZERS

1. Maria Shriver, *The Shriver Report: A Woman's Nation Changes Everything* (Washington D.C.: Center for American Progress, 2009), 1–2.

2. Warren Farrell, *The Myth of Male Power: Why Men Are the Disposable Sex* (New York: Berkley Books, 1993), 351.

3. Phyllis Schlafly, *The Power of the Positive Woman* (New Rochelle, NY: Arlington Publishers, 1977), 9.

CHAPTER 1: BRAINWASHED

1. Nancy Gibbs, "What Women Want Now," *Time* (October 14, 2009).

2. Betsey Stevenson and Justin Wolfers, *Paradox of Declining Female Happiness* (New Haven, CT: American Law and Economics Association, 2008).

3. Betty Friedan, *The Feminine Mystique* (New York: W. W. Norton & Company, 2001), xv.

4. Maria Shriver, *The Shriver Report: A Woman's Nation Changes Everything* (Washington D.C.: Center for American Progress, 2009), iv.

5. Ibid, 15

6. Barack Obama, interview by Savannah Guthrie, *NBC News*, October 21, 2009.

7. David Horowitz, *One-Party Classroom: How Radical Professors at America's Top Colleges Indoctrinate Students and Undermine Our Democracy* (New York: Crown, 2009), 209.

8. Ibid., 210.

9. Ibid., 212.

10. Megan Basham, *Beside Every Successful Man: Getting the Life You Want by Helping Your Husband Get Ahead* (New York: Three Rivers Press, 2009), 7.

11. Dr. Jean M. Twenge, *Generation Me: Why Today's Young Americans Are More Confident, Assertive, Entitled—and More Miserable Than Ever Before* (New York: Free Press, 2007), 34.

12. Jessica Valenti, "For women in America, equality is still an illusion," *Washington Post*, Feb. 21, 2010, http://www.washingtonpost.com/wp-dyn/content/article/2010/02/19/AR2010021902049.html.

13. Amy Richards as told to Amy Barrett, "LIVES; When One Is Enough," *New York Times Magazine*, July 18, 2004, http://www.nytimes.com/2004/07/18/magazine/lives-when-one-is-enough.html.

14. Ibid.

15. Andrea Wong and Rosario Dawson, *Secrets of Powerful Women: Leading Change for a New Generation* (New York: Hyperion, 2010), xi.

16. Ibid., 52.

17. Myrna Blyth, *Spin Sisters: How the Women of the Media Sell Unhappiness and Liberalism to the Women of America* (New York: St. Martin's Press, 2004), 4.

18. Bernard Goldberg, *Arrogance: Rescuing America from the Media Elite* (New York: Warner Books, 2003), 128.

19. Gloria Steinem, interview by Campbell Brown, *CNN Election Center*, June 9, 2008; transcripts at http://archives.cnn.com/TRANSCRIPTS/0806/09/ec.01.html.

20. Kate O'Beirne, *Women Who Make the World Worse: (and How Their Radical Feminist Assault Is Ruining Our Schools, Families, Military, and Sports)* (New York: Sentinel, 2006), xv.

21. Goldberg, *Arrogance*, 128.

22. Gloria Steinem, "Leaps of Consciousness," keynote speech, Women and Power Conference, September 2004, http://www.feminist.com/resources/artspeech/genwom/leaps.html.

23. Steven Rhoads, *Taking Sex Differences Seriously* (New York: Encounter Books, 2004), 5.

24. Jessica Valenti, "Opinion: The fake feminism of Sarah Palin," *Washington Post*, May 30, 2010, http:www.washingtonpost.com/wp-dyn/content/article/2010/05/28/AR2010052802263.html?sid=ST2010062204464.

CHAPTER 2: FEMINISM 101: UNCENSORED

1. Betty Friedan, *The Feminine Mystique* (New York: W. W. Norton & Company, 2001), 314, 336.

2. Kathleen Parker, *Save the Males: Why Men Matter[,] Why Women Should Care* (New York: Random House, 2008), 196.

3. Friedan, *The Feminine Mystique*, 337.

4. Cheryl Saban, *What Is Your Self-Worth? A Woman's Guide to Validation* (New York: Hay House, 2009), xxi.

5. Kate O'Beirne, *Women Who Make the World Worse: (and How Their Radical Feminist Assault Is Ruining Our Schools, Families, Military, and Sports)* (New York: Sentinel, 2006), xix.

6. F. Carolyn Graglia, *Domestic Tranquility: A Brief Against Feminism* (Dallas: Spence Publishing, 2008), 19.

7. Ibid., 18.

8. Jean Williams, "Heavy Investment of Time Required for Broker's Trade," *St. Louis Post-Dispatch* (July 15, 1966).

9. Ibid.

10. Midge Decter, *An Old Wife's Tale: My Seven Decades in Love and War* (New York: Regan Books, 2001), 70.

11. Betty Friedan, *Life So Far: A Memoir* (New York: Simon & Schuster, 2006), 26, 121, 131.

12. Freidan, *The Feminine Mystique*, 381.

13. *Sex Bias in the U.S. Code* (Washington, D.C.: United States Commission on Civil Rights, April 1977).

14. Barbara A. Brown, et al, "The Equal Rights Amendment: A Constitutional Basis for Equal Rights for Women," *Yale Law Journal*, 80, no. 5 (April 1971): 871–985, http://www.jstor.org/stable/795228.

15. O'Beirne, *Women Who Make the World Worse*, xiv.

16. Gloria Steinem, interview in the documentary "No Safe Place: Violence Against Women," aired on PBS (March 27, 1998).

17. Ibid.

18. Louann Brizendine, *The Male Brain: A Breakthrough Understanding of How Men and Boys Think* (New York: Broadway Books, 2010), 4, 18.

19. Ibid., 21.

20. George Gilder, *Men and Marriage* (Gretna, LA: Pelican Publishing, 1992), 11.

21. Simone de Beauvoir, interview with Betty Friedan (1976), quoted in Mona Charen, *Do-Gooders—How Liberals Hurt Those They Claim to Help* (New York: Sentinel, 2004), 124.

22. Linda Hirshman interview by Diane Sawyer, "How to Raise Kids: Stay Home or Go to Work?" *Good Morning America*, February 23, 2006.

23. Annie Groer, "The Girls in the House," *More*, March 2010, http://www.more.com/2050/12386-dc-power-women-roommates.

24. Ibid.

25. Susan Toepfer, "Did Feminism Make Women Miserable?" *Speakeasy* (blog), *Wall Street Journal*, April 21, 2010, http://blogs.wsj.com/speakeasy/2010/04/21/did-feminism-make-women-miserable-naomi-wolf-responds/.

26. Andre Harper, *Political Emancipation: Observations from a Black Man Who Rejected Liberal Indoctrination* (Morgan Hill, CA: Bookstand Publishing, 2009), 11.

27. Maria Shriver, *The Shriver Report: A Woman's Nation Changes Everything* (Washington, D.C.: Center for American Progress, 2009).

28. "Necessary Compromises: How Parents, Employers and Children's Advocates View Child Care Today," Public Agenda, 2000.

29. Dr. Jean M. Twenge, *Generation Me: Why Today's Young Americans Are More Confident, Assertive, Entitled—and More Miserable Than Ever Before* (New York: Free Press, 2007), 34.

30. Ralph G. Martin, "Kate Hepburn: My Life & Loves," *Ladies' Home Journal* (August 1975): 102–3.

31. Dinesh D'Souza, *Letters to a Young Conservative* (New York: Basic Books, 2002), 104.

32. Ibid., 105.

33. Naomi Wolf, "What Price Happiness" (lecture at luncheon honoring Wolf, *More* magazine, New York, NY, April 2010).

34. Warren Farrell, *The Myth of Male Power: Why Men Are the Disposable Sex* (New York: Berkley Books, 1993), 40.

CHAPTER 3: HOOKUPS AND HEARTACHE

1. F. Carolyn Graglia, *Domestic Tranquility: A Brief Against Feminism* (Dallas: Spence Publishing, 1998), 7.

2. Dr. Miriam Grossman, *Unprotected: A Campus Psychiatrist Reveals How Political Correctness in Her Profession Endangers Every Student* (New York: Sentinel, 2007), xvi.

3. Dr. Miriam Grossman, "UN Commission on the Status of Women" (lecture, Millenium Plaza Hotel, New York, NY, March 8, 2010).

4. Dinesh D'Souza, *Letters to a Young Conservative* (New York: Basic Books, 2002), 4.

5. Dr. Jean M. Twenge, *Generation Me: Why Today's Young Americans Are More Confident, Assertive, Entitled—and More Miserable Than Ever Before* (New York: Free Press, 2007), 20.

6. P. J. O'Rourke, interview by Tom Brokaw, "Boomer$!" CNBC, March 4, 2010.

7. Grossman, *Unprotected*, 3.

8. Stephanie Chen, "No hooking up, no sex for some coeds," *CNN*

Living, April 19, 2010, http://www.cnn.com/2010/LIVING/04/19/college.anti.hookup.culture/index.html.

9. Kerry Cohen, *Loose Girl: A Memoir of Promiscuity* (New York: Hyperion, 2008), 3.

10. Ibid., 2.

11. Dr. Miriam Grossman, "The Dangers of Social Ideology in Campus Health Care," *Policy Express*, no. 7-2, Clare Boothe Luce Policy Institute.

12. Dr. Laura Berman, "The Sex Ed Handbook: A Comprehensive Guide for Parents" (2009), 9, http://media.oprah.com/lberman/talking-to-kids-about-sex-handbook.pdf.

13. Jean M. Twenge, and W. Keith Campbell, *The Narcissism Epidemic: Living in the Age of Entitlement* (New York: Free Press, 2010), 85.

14. Wendy Shalit, *The Good Girl Revolution: Young Rebels with Self-Esteem and High Standards* (New York: Ballantine Books, 2008), 278.

15. Caitlin Flanagan, "Love, Actually," *Atlantic*, June 2010, http://www.theatlantic.com/magazine/archive/2010/06/love-actually/8094/.

16. Dr. Miriam Grossman. *You're Teaching My Child What? A Physician Exposes the Lies of Sex Education and How They Harm Your Child* (Washington D.C.: Regnery Publishing, 2010), 183.

17. Shalit, *The Good Girl Revolution*, 11.

CHAPTER 4: WHY MARRIAGE ELUDES THE
MODERN GENERATION

1. Pamela Paul, *The Starter Marriage and the Future of Matrimony* (New York: Random House, 2002), viii.

2. Sharon Jayson, "Couples take their sweet time," *USA Today*, June 22, 2010, 1D.

3. M. Scott Peck, *The Road Less Traveled* (New York: Simon & Schuster, 1978), 85.

4. Ibid.

5. Judith S. Wallerstein and Sandra Blakeslee, *The Good Marriage: How and Why Love Lasts* (New York: Warner Books, 1995), 7.

6. Beth Frerking, *Secrets of Powerful Women: Leading Change for a New Generation* (New York: Hyperion, 2010), 181.

7. George Gilder, *Men and Marriage* (Gretna, LA:, Pelican Publishing, 1992), 14.

8. Sandra Bullock, interview by Barbara Walters, "Barbara Walters' Oscar Night Special," ABC, March 7, 2010.

9. Vicki Iovine, "Tipper and Al Separate: Congratulations to Them," *Huffington Post* (June 4, 2010), http://www.huffingtonpost.com/vicki-iovine/girlfriends-guide-tipper_b_600185.html.

10. Ellen Tien, "Confessions of a Semi-Happy Wife," *O: The Oprah Magazine*, May 1, 2008, http://www.oprah.com/relationships/Dreaming-of-Divorce-Ellen-Tiens-Mid-Wife-Crisis/1.

11. Ibid.

12. Ellen McCarthy, "Profile of Elizabeth Gilbert," *Washington Post*, January 7, 2010, http://www.washingtonpost.com/wp-dyn/content/article/2010/01/06/AR2010010604769.html.

13. Ibid.

14. Kitty Kelley, *Oprah, A Biography* (New York: Crown Publishers, 2010), 160.

15. Elizabeth Gilbert interview by Lucy Kaylin, *O: The Oprah Magazine*, December 14, 2009.

16. Myrna Blyth, *Spin Sisters: How the Women of the Media Sell Unhappiness and Liberalism to the Women of America* (New York: St. Martin's Press, 2004), vii.

17. Kelley, *Oprah*, 189.

18. Elizabeth Gilbert, *Committed: A Skeptic Makes Peace with Marriage* (New York: Viking, 2010), 42.

19. Elizabeth Gilbert, *Eat, Pray, Love* (New York: Penguin, 2006), 17.

20. Caitlin Flanagan, "Why Marriage Matters," *Time,* July 13, 2009: 46.

21. Justin Lahart and Emmeline Zhao, "What Would You Do with an Extra Hour?" June 23, 2010.

22. Barry Schwartz, *The Paradox of Choice: Why Less Is More* (New York: Harper Collins, 2004), 228.

23. George Gilder, *Men and Marriage* (Gretna, LA: Pelican Publishing, 1992), 5.

24. Michael Noer, "Don't Marry Career Women," *Forbes,* August 22, 2006, http://www.forbes.com/2006/08/23/Marriage-Careers-Divorce_cx_mn_land.html.

25. Ibid.

26. http://www.amazon.com/Marry-Him-Case-Setting-Enough/product-reviews/0525951512.

27. Betsey Stevenson and Justin Wolfers, *The Paradox of Declining Female Happiness* (New Haven, CT: American Law and Economics Association, 2009).

28. Raquel Welch, *Raquel: Beyond the Cleavage* (New York: Weinstein Books, 2010), 191.

29. Po Bronson and Ashley Merryman, *Nurtureshock: New Thinking about Children* (New York: Twelve, 2009), 9.

30. Lori Gottleib to Sara Lipka, "The Case for Mr. Not-Quite-Right," *Atlantic,* February 2008.

CHAPTER 5: WHEN MOTHERS WORK

1. William and Wendy Dreskin, *The Day Care Decision: What's Best for You and Your Child* (New York: M. Evans & Co., 1983), 31.

2. Bernard Goldberg, *Bias: A CBS Insider Exposes How the Media Distort the News* (Washington, D.C.: Regnery, 2002), 166.

3. Dave Crenshaw, *The Myth of Multitasking: How Doing It All Gets Nothing Done* (New York: Jossey-Bass, 2008), 30.

4. Lisa Belkin, "The Opt-Out Revolution," *New York Times,* October 26, 2003.

5. Inara Verzemnieks, "Will My Child Turn Out Okay?" *Working Mother,* May 2010, 92.

6. Ilisa Cohen, "Anatomy of Working Mother Guilt," *Working Mother* June/July 2010, http://www.workingmother.com/web? service =direct/1/ViewRotatingPortlent/RotatingPortalBlocks/dlinkArticle &sp=S3193&sp=118.

7. Suzanne Riss, "The Biggest Loser's Alison Sweeney," *Working Mother*, May 2010, 44.

8. Alicia Ybarco and Mary Ann Zoellner, "Today Show Moms," *Cookie*, May 2009.

9. Cathy L. Greenberg, PhD, and Barrett S. Avigdor, JD *What Happy Working Mothers Know* (New York: Wiley, 2009), 78.

10. Campbell Brown, "Campbell Brown to Leave CNN" Media Decoder (blog), *New York Times*, May 18, 2010, http://mediadecoder .blogs.nytimes.com/2010/05/18/campbell-brown-to-leave-cnn/.

11. Katherine Heigl to Michael Ausiello, "The Goodbye Girl," *Entertainment Weekly*, April 2, 2010, 33.

12. Bridget Brennan, *Why She Buys: The New Strategy for Reaching the World's Most Powerful Consumers* (New York: Crown Business, 2009), 30–31.

13. Ibid.

14. Ibid.

15. Megan McArdle, "Misleading Indicator," *Atlantic*, November 2009, 37.

16. David Gelernter, "Why Mothers Should Stay Home," *Commentary*, February 1996, http://www.commentarymagazine.com/ viewarticle.cfm/why-mothers-should-stay-home-8520.

17. Graglia, *Domestic Tranquility*, 2, 27.

18. Katrina Alcorn, "How does The Man do it?" Working Moms Break blog, March 19, 2010, http://www.workingmomsbreak.com/ 2010/03/19/how-does-the-man-do-it/.

19. Daniela Drake and Elizabeth Ford, *Smart Girls Marry Money: How Women Are Getting Shafted by Their Romantic Expectations and What They Can Do About It* (Philadelphia: Running Press, 2010), 9.

20. Kim Parker, "The Harried Life of the Working Mother," Pew Research Center, October 1, 2009, http://www.pewresearch.org/ pubs/1360/working-women-conflicted-but-few-favor-return-to-tra-ditional-roles.

21. Sue Shellenbarger, "Therapy in Preschools: Can It Have Lasting Benefits?" *Wall Street Journal*, September 8, 2009, http://

online.wsj.com/article/SB10001424052970204348804574400612
690410766.html.

22. Ibid.

23. Ibid.

24. Ibid.

25. Judith S. Wallerstein, Julia M. Lewis, Sandra Blakeslee, *The Unexpected Legacy of Divorce: A 25 Year Landmark Study* (New York: Hyperion, 2000), xxii.

26. "Education" Organizing for America Web site, accessed August 23, 2010, http://www.barackobama.com/issues/education/.

27. Shellenbarger, "Therapy in Preschools.

28. Diane Fisher, "Pre to Three: Policy Implications of Child Brain Development" Congressional Testimony (June 5, 1997).

CHAPTER 6: PANDERING TO THE FEMALE LEFT— AT YOUR EXPENSE

1. Resolution B-1, adopted at the National Education Association Convention in New Orleans, 2010.

2. Ibid.

3. Dr. Byron White, quoted in Phyllis Schlafly, *Who Will Rock the Cradle?* (Washington D.C.: Eagle Forum Education Fund, 1989), 20.

4. David Elkind, *The Hurried Child: Growing Up Too Fast Too Soon* (New York: Da Capo, 2001), 32.

5. Leslie Bennetts, "The New Push for Quality Child Care," *Parade*, July 19, 2009, 4.

6. Ibid.

7. Diane Fisher, "Pre to Three: Policy Implications of Child Brain Development" Congressional Testimony (June 5, 1997).

8. Karl Zinsmeister, "The Problem with Day Care," *American Enterprise*, May/June 1998.

9. White House Statement by the President on Equal Pay, July 20, 2010, quoted in Diana Furchtgott-Roth, "'Paycheck Fairness' is anything but," *Examiner*, http://www.washingtonexaminer.com/opinion/

columns/_Paycheck-Fairness_-is-anything-but-1002855-99061249.
html.

10. The Federal Budget, Fiscal Year 2011.

11. Ruth Bader Ginsburg, *Sex Bias in the U.S. Code: A Report of the United States Commission on Civil Rights*, April 1977, 206.

12. Barack Obama, speech to Planned Parenthood, "Barack Obama Promises to Sign FOCA," July 9, 2008, http://www.you tube.com/watch?v=pf0XIRZSTt8.

13. Liz Weiss and Page Gardner, *Advancing the Economic Security of Unmarried Women* (Washington, D.C., Center for American Progress, March 2010), 1.

CHAPTER 7: THE EXPENDABLE MALE

1. Mary-Louise Parker, interview by Meryl Gordon, "Parker's Progress," *More*, June 2009, 147.

2. Natalie Angier, "The Male of the Species: Why Is He Needed?" *New York Times*, May 17, 1994.

3. "Are Men Necessary?" *CNN.com*, November 15, 2005, http://www.cnn.com/2005/SHOWBIZ/books/11/15/dowd.men.necessary/index.html.

4. Katie Couric to Nicole Contos, *The Today Show*, 1997.

5. Lisa Belkin, "Are Men Necessary?" Motherlode: Adventures in Parenting blog, *New York Times Magazine*, June 30, 2010, http://parenting.blogs.nytimes.com/2010/06/30/are-men-necessary/.

6. Pamela Paul, "Are Fathers Necessary?" *Atlantic*, July/August 2010, http://www.theatlantic.com/magazine/archive/2010/07/are-fathers-necessary/8136/.

7. Bernard Goldberg, *Bias: A CBS Insider Exposes Media Bias* (Washington D.C.: Regnery, 2004), 135.

8. Larry Summers, "Differences between the Sexes," Conference on Diversifying the Science and Engineering Workforce (January 2005).

9. Margaret Hoover interview by Bill O'Reilly, Fox News, *The O'Reilly Factor*, March 23, 2009.

10. Ibid.

11. Alexis Chiu et al, "Jennifer Aniston Ready for a Baby?" *People*, August 23, 2010, 62.

12. Kathleen Parker, *Save the Males: Why Men Matter [,] Why Women Should Care* (New York: Random House, 2008), 4.

13. Edith Green, "The Road Is Paved with Good Intentions," address at Brigham Young University (January 25, 1977).

14. Hanna Rosin, "The End of Men," *The Atlantic*, June/July 2010, http://www.theatlantic.com/magazine/archive/2010/07/the-end-of-men/8135/.

15. Warren Farrell, *The Myth of Male Power: Why Men Are the Disposable Sex* (New York: Berkley Books, 1993), 292.

16. Judge Robert H. Dierker Jr., *The Tyranny of Tolerance: A Sitting Judge Breaks the Code of Silence to Expose the Liberal Judicial Assault* (New York: Crown Forum, 2006), 13.

17. Laura Sessions Stepp, "A New Kind of Date Rape," *Cosmopolitan*, September 2007, http://www.cosmopolitan.com/sex-love/tips-moves/new-kind-of-date-rape.

18. George Gilder, *Men and Marriage* (Louisiana, Pelican Publishing, 1992), 14.

19. Aisha Sultan, "Who's the boss at home?" *St. Louis Post-Dispatch,* May 22, 2010, L7.

20. Ibid.

21. Louann Brizendine, *The Male Brain: A Breakthrough Understanding of How Men and Boys Think* (New York: Broadway Books, 2010), 5.

22. Beth Hale, "What women want in 2010: A husband who'll be the main breadwinner," *Mail Online*, July 13, 2010, http://www.dailymail.co.uk/news/article-1251873/What-women-want-2010-A-husband-wholl-main-breadwinner.html.

23. Brizendine, *The Male Brain*, 91.

24. Stephen Baskerville, *Taken into Custody: The War against Fatherhood, Marriage, and the Family* (Nashville: Cumberland House Publishing, 2007), 112.

25. Michael Reagan, *Twice Adopted: An Important Social*

Commentator Speaks to the Cultural Ailments Threatening America Today (Nashville: B&H Books, 2004), 44.

26. Todd M. Aglialoro, "The Government, Divorce, and the War on Fatherhood," *InsideCatholic*, December 5, 2008.

27. Goldberg, *Bias*, 136.

28. F. Carolyn Graglia, *Domestic Tranquility: A Brief against Feminism* (Dallas: Spence Publishing, 1998), 88.

29. Reb Bradley, *Born Liberal, Raised Right: How to Rescue America from Moral Decline—One Family at a Time* (Los Angeles/WND Books, 2008), xiii.

30. Ibid., 139.

CHAPTER 8: A NEW ROADMAP FOR WOMEN

1. Raymond Lloyd Richmond, "A Guide to Psychology and Its Practice," http://www.guidetopsychology.com/txtypes.htm

2. Jean M. Twenge, *Generation Me: Why Today's Young Americans Are More Confident, Assertive, Entitled—and More Miserable Than Ever Before* (New York: Free Press, 2007), 201.

3. Dinesh D'Souza, *Letters to a Young Conservative* (New York: Basic Books, 2002), 10.

4. Anne Taylor Fleming, *Motherhood Deferred: A Woman's Journey* (Darby, PA: Diane Publishing Co., 1994).

5. Premier issue of *Aura*, a British magazine, 2000

6. Rebecca Walker, "How my mother's fanatical views tore us apart," *Mail Online* (UK), http://www.dailymail.co.uk/femail/article-1021293/How-mothers-fanatical-feminist-views-tore-apart-daughter-The-Color-Purple-author.html.

7. Maria Shriver, *The Shriver Report* (Washington, D.C.: Center for American Progress, 2009).

8. Barry Schwartz, *The Paradox of Choice: Why More Is Less* (New York: Harper Collins, 2004), 145.

9. Clare Boothe Luce, "Points to Ponder," *Reader's Digest*, March 26, 1996, 32.

10. Midge Decter, *An Old Wife's Tale: My Seven Decades in Love and War* (New York: Regan Books, 2001), 193.

11. Peter Berkowitz, "The Death of Conservatism Was Greatly Exaggerated," *Wall Street Journal,* August 28, 2010, A13.

12. Lisa Belkin, "The Opt-Out Revolution," *New York Times,* Oct. 26, 2003.

13. F. Carolyn Graglia, *Domestic Tranquility: A Brief Against Feminism* (Dallas: Spence Publishing, 1998), 25.

APPENDIX C

1. *National NOW Times,* Fall 1990 and Summer 1991.

INDEX